Adrift

Adrift

Jack Foley

"Tell me what, tell me what can I do?—
I'm a drift in this world without you."

PANTOGRAPH PRESS

Published in the United States by Pantograph Press, P.O. Box 9643 Berkeley, CA 94709.

Complete versions or portions of these poems have appeared in *Angel Island, Barque, The Beloit Poetry Journal, Brief, Caveat Lector, The Fiction Review, MODOM, NRG, Outré, Poetry USA, Shock's Bridge, Talisman,* and *Tight.*
Judy Patton performed a dance to my taped recitation of "Sweeney Adrift," and "The Tiger" and various passages from this book were heard on KPFA radio. Glenn Spearman's sax and Benjamin Lindgren's bass added considerably to the effectiveness of the radio presentation.

Special thanks to my wife Adelle for her enthusiasm, performance skills, perseverence, cheer & love.

Library of Congress Cataloging-in-Publication Data
Foley, Jack, 1940-
Adrift / Jack Foley. — 1st ed.
p. cm.
ISBN 1-880766-05-1 : $8.95
I. Title.
PS3556.03915A65 1993
811'.54—dc20 93-1442
CIP

This book is dedicated to my wife Adelle and my son Sean

"One decisive test turns on the age of the ocean floor.
If the continents have been fixed, the ocean basins should all be as old as the continents. If drift has occurred, some regions of the ocean floor should be younger than the drift."

— J. Tuzo Wilson
Continental Drift

The Mind, that Ocean where each kind
Does streight its own resemblance find;
Yet it creates, transcending these,
Far other Worlds, and other Seas...

— Andrew Marvell
The Garden

CONTENTS

SWEENEY ADRIFT

"Apeneck Sweeney spreads his knees...."
— T. S. Eliot

"How is it possible to write one's autobiography in a world so fast-changing as this?"
"My whole life had been a chronology of – *changes.*"
— *The Autobiography of Malcolm X*

for my friend, Ivan Argüelles, *sine quo non*

Argüelles and I were speaking about the way in which the theme, the topos, of the descent into the dead is enormously important in 20th-century literature. One finds it in many of the "classics" of modernism: Eliot's *Waste Land,* Joyce's *Ulysses,* Pound's *Cantos,* Yeats, so on and so forth. It's an Orphic theme, and one can discover it not only in Homer but in "numerous stories occurring in the mythology and folklore of every people in the world, ancient and contemporary" (Funk & Wagnalls' *Standard Dictionary*). One might think of it as a kind of *welcome to the house...*

welcome to the house of failure
see these are the structural bases of the house its beams and arteries
its artificial light its hands its vast appendices
who is
not here?
the range of things
delights us welcome welcome

see there is the door it opens for us
welcome

what sweeney what
have you done and
where have you done it?
sweeney clubbed the man
not once but twice; bashed his head in, hurt
him badly. Oh,
Sweeney they'll
not stand for that surely—
surely that's
no way to behave—
Sweeney
ended his tirade
his wild life then—
They all said, Enough, enough, Sweeney,

cf. *Buile Suibhne*
trans. J.G. O'Keefe, 1913
trans. Seamus Heaney, 1984

surely that's
no way
for a man to behave
Sweeney
kicked his eyes out hurt him broke his ribs twisted the tongue not once
but twice
bones broke, brittle for Sweeney, his trophy, taken, the life taken, the
balls
bashed,
the life
ended
oh Sweeney
she bespoke him sorely oh
and sweeney repented then
turned churchman spoke vows made retreats novenas bled holy water
ended his wild life
told tales made miracles believed end-
ed his wild life turned goodman churchman died of age and
soul
now surely turned—
to
heav'n.
sweeney.

SUN-

the slow turn of resolving
  moved (as ever) us (as ever) if
  (stay)

I go out again with
  money in my pockets

click!

how many times have I
asked you—spoken your
name—in this darkness—
I have nothing to offer—
in the air—endless
variations—*speech!*—

Bear
  turns—
open to the
 light—

She stopped for a moment and looked back. It is not easy to tell. They saw each other only momentarily. It was not easy to tell.

Your book is...

a big crazy delicious effort, fundamentally great, highly interesting, jocular, kinky, lovely, magnificently nice, opulent, pretty, quick, redolent, snazzy, tricky, undoubtedly very whimsical Xmas yummy. Zounds!

The night came, and a storm, and Sweeney's misery and mania were so great that he cried out:

I who have neither another nor now
in the dim light (love)
possibly
frame (make) this (how) (love) quick

"I wrow rowe wrote chu
yesterday"—

Sweeney returns, and the lies about his son's death have caused him to

All day, all night,
Sweeney clings
to the branch, and opens
(spreads his)
wings

He is now
"adrift"—

(spoken to—
uneasy in the night—
pressure—)

Remember this, "friend"—
hand extended—

is the problem presence?
what does it matter if we love each other?
is the problem presence?
what does it matter if we love each other?
is the problem presence?
what does it matter if we love each other?
is the problem presence?
what does it matter if we love each other?

bear
   the bear-son
opes
   his eyes

the "master of the mountain" is of special interest to us as he is the "master" of the bears. On the one hand, he is a man, on the other, a real bear, only of unusually large size. All other bears are his fellow tribesmen...The slaughter of a bear represents the departure of the soul of the animal to its master and a subsequent return to earth is expected...It is not to the beasts themselves that offerings and prayers are made but to their "masters" or "owners"

"grandfather"..."old man"..."he"...Taking the skin off a slain bear they say, "Grandfather, owner of the earth, don't think ill of us. We did not do this to you. The Yakut did it. Your silver bones we shall put in a special house."

fish-dragon
blind and eyeless
naked as a
human finger
Sweeney

pueblo—bridge—creek—
cameras
clicking—old woman—looking—
eyes: thinking—

"We're going to have lunch with the guy who published *Nailed to the Coffin of Life.* His name is Loss Glazier."
"His name is Loss?"   "Lunch With Loss"
"Yes."
"We're going to have lunch with Loss?"
"Yes."
"I've been having Lunch with Loss for most of my life."

the bear has always been the weather prophet because he presages by his
emergence the
return of spring
to the
wintry
world
Juan, Juan el Oso, Juan del Oso, Ivanko the Bear's son—

Since matter itself is in a state of flux and is deprived of that form through which it takes shape and is made manifest, they took the dampness and humidity of caves, their darkness, and, as the poet says, their "murkiness," as an appropriate symbol for the properties of the cosmos

the Persian mystagogues initiate their candidate by explaining to him the downward journey of souls and their subsequent return, and they call the place where this occurs a "cave"—

descending paralysis
bull
lord of *genesis*

sun—
          shadow—

there is
blood on my face—

fuck it you know that fuckin cocksucker you know what that fucker said to me

Sweeney picked himself up off the hardbitterdesolatefrozen ground. Again.

"Mother, would you *please* answer the door. I've been standing here for fifteen minutes."
"Couldn't be helped. I was on the shitter."

—neighborhood music

what does it mean to use the word fuck?

"Sleep a little, love,
                    for thou needst not fear the least"—

"I am Sweeney alas!
my wretched body is utterly dead—
A year have I been on the mountain
  without music, without sleep—
Madman
          am I—"

John Anson wrote a hundred rounds
As I have written only one.
O listen as his name resounds:
          John Anson.

My little round might be the sun.
The planets in their daily rounds
Must circle it in unison.

around the roundel

His trope might be the separate gowns
Of long-dead ladies now at one.
These separated, joining sounds:
John—
Ann's son.

how many times have I
asked you—spoken your
name—in this darkness—
I have nothing to offer—
in the air—endless
variations—speech—

It was night. The heat was still glutinous and no wind stirred. The whirling "deedees" died away to the east as the glowing orange orb of the sun drifted to the west in a purple miasma. (A narrative of *ideas* not of *events.*)

And, Orpheus, will you bring your mother with you?—

field piece violence cob decoration porcupine brogan finch zeppelin permeate convent artefact behemoth climax ranger pin mens rea brand convent jitter own as bell man scatter which saddle strange blend peace orphan spatch poll boing infant such enter hone savor claim once ping
Rhea—

—Why have you followed me here?
—*Yes.*
—What have you come to tell me?
—*Yes!*

(Here the Hag speaketh
with Sweeney
and telleth him
nothing.)

THE DEEP AND ABIDING MISERY OF THE MAD!
it was all sorrows love's seeking
in a bloodless ending still steeping
Sorrow, be neither stow(n)e nor still
it was blunt weeping
—The fly Augusta, the little imp
teases your nose and your forehead.
When one is a fly one is not an eagle
but one knows how to walk on the ceiling.
Pierre Febvre...Yes, Pierre Febvre. Why should I not think of him, and

wonder what my spirit will make of him, feeling as I now do. His face—
O obstinate mysteries,
innocent animality!
You, simple house-fly
and you—foxes, crows, panthers,
creatures in whom the impulse to bite exuberates—
But I understand now how it is possible to muse upon the outline of a nostril or the curve of a lip for hour upon hour and never be satisfied.
Ha! Ha! Ha! Difference of sex makes for clear-sightedness, eh?
The street was dark; the Square was deserted;
the morning sun was still
and did not rise. "Sweeney—?"
Nevertheless I spent less time on the opening caresses in order to get to the concluding ones with which we had just become acquainted.
I lie upon the grass and see the sky. Her dress
billowed in the wind.
He sits for hours staring at the sea.
The way your breasts move as you move—the strangeness of it
It is the woman's part
to touch the
hand
to let you know she *wishes* to be touched—
August-
a thrives in the summer's carrion—
The relationship
between the self-discovering mind and the world,
between the self-discovering mind and others, is one of *analogy*. I can "find" myself not by looking inward but by looking outward (invidia, envy, mania)
He stared upon the table on which a knife a fork and a spoon had been carefully arranged
There are, uh, times I forget
I meant to
to forget
times I do not want to
to
remember
"It's possible he has another reason for acting as he does. It's possible he genuinely has something to hide."

—Dawn light
mechanical and
human figures
catch the light

Think not, revolted Spirit, thy shape the same,
Or undiminisht brightness, to be known
As when thou stood'st in Heav'n upright and pure (thrives in the summer's carrion)
sunlight? here?   through a single
shaft
What are the names of the Seven Dwarfs?
Slothful, Envious, Lustful, Wrathful, Shameless...
contradictions   explanations
you who turn the wheel—

— loneliness at the
shopping mall

[...an immense Being who alone remains eternal amidst the continual change and ceaseless transformation of all that constitutes him...]

are you as good at sex as you are at literature?

For he whose mind is fixed upon true being has surely no time to look down upon the affairs of earth or to be filled with malice and envy, contending against men; his eye is ever directed towards things fixed and immutable, which he sees neither injuring nor injured by one another, but all in order moving according to reason; these he imitates, and to these he will, as far as he can, conform himself.

—you complain about "obscurity"
and assert that my poetry
is overly "intellectual."
You assume in saying this
that however complicated
"intellectual"
matters may be, in matters of
"emotion"
you stand with the poet
on common ground.
But is it not possible
that the poet has
felt something which you have not yet
felt
or have not yet recognized as
feeling,
that it is an emotional
not an intellectual
"obscurity"
to which you object?

And now, I said, let me show in a figure how far our nature is enlightened or unenlightened. Imagine mankind living in a cave with a long entrance open to the light; in this they have been since childhood.

A "friend" is a relative. To "have right" expresses obligation. About half the families have horse-drawn mowing machines. Those who have them mow their own meadows, working from earliest morning as long as light holds. They work with the aid of their sons and of boys from the families which have no machines. At each stage of the process a boy not a member of the family gives his labour and takes his place at meals during the day.

"I am patriotic and it may be a bad thing to say but I think that the school system they have now is bad and that the teaching of Irish is bad. In my day and before, a man might go to school when he could— maybe for only three months in the year. But he would know more then than they get now when they go to school all the time. The old people learned more then too. When a child finished school he would be expected to read a newspaper to the old people or to write a letter for them or to do sums. And he would do it well." ...a system which to his mind makes no provision for the mutuality between young and old...

and when one of them is liberated and compelled suddenly to stand up and turn his neck round and walk and look towards the light he will suffer sharp pains; the glare will distress him, and he will be unable to see the realities of what in his former state he had seen only as shadows

Things are "CAST ADRIFT,"
more or less like one another without any of them being able to claim the privileged status of "model" for all the rest—

Sweeney moved amongst the branches making a tremendous sound in the / head which listens

How is talk measured, love— Beyond the obvious—
"stained" words—
restrained—
heart's clue
spoken

"Continual changes...are...every instant...occurring...to every...man"

"...I would never have by myself undertaken the task of establishing such a collection and, grateful as I am to Bill Germano for his initiative, I confess that I still look back upon it with some misgivings. Such massive evidence of the failure to make the various individual readings coalesce is a somewhat melancholy spectacle. The fragmentary aspect of the whole is made more obvious still by the hypotactic manner that prevails in each of the essays taken in isolation, by the continued attempt, however ironized, to present a closed and linear argument. This apparent coherence *within* each essay is not matched by a corresponding coherence *between* them. Laid out diachronically in a roughly chronological sequence, they do not evolve in a manner that easily allows for dialectical progression or, ultimately, for historical totalization. Rather, it seems that they always start again from scratch and that their conclusions fail to add up to anything. If some secret principle of summation is at work here, I do not feel qualified to articulate it and, as far as the general question of romanticism is concerned, I must leave the task of its historical definition to others. I have myself taken refuge in more theoretical inquiries into the problems of figural language. Not that I believe that such a historical enterprise, in the case of romanticism, is doomed from the start: one is all too easily tempted to rationalize personal shortcoming as theoretical impossibility and, especially among younger scholars, there is ample evidence that the historical study of romanticism is being successfully pursued. But it certainly has become a far from easy task. One feels at times envious of those who can continue to do literary history as if nothing had happened in the sphere of theory, but one cannot help but feel somewhat suspicious of their optimism. *The Rhetoric of Romanticism* should at least help to document some of the difficulties it fails to resolve...." (Paul de Man, 1983)

Los Angeles, by its absence
dominates everything—
Sharp-eyed lynxes
watch us: Goyim?

How can one
begin

To think of you I
move

        "Hello, Tiny"

In the evening, in the rain—
        of birds
        a harvest-
                wealth-

CHORUS: SON(G)

for Jake Berry

this piece was written to be performed by my wife Adelle and myself

beginning
his first consciousness/was an immense nostalgia—an awareness/of
"passage"—
the universe is running down—always in the direction of increasing entropy
the brutality of the word "tu-meur" be careful here is intelligence at work
self-hatred masochism —he spoke of the dog as "dominant"—
it would be necessary to give a full account of the present state of the public taste in this country, and to determine how far this taste is healthy or depraved; which, again, could not be determined without pointing out in what manner language and the human mind act and re-act on each other, and without retracing the revolutions, not of literature alone, but likewise of society itself. —What of all these
"voices?"
the language poet orders "tongue"—
how can we look
to words?—how can we look?—the two
of us
stranded, touching, telling—
"I'm just beginning to reach the point where I—"
-what you're objecting to in my poem is not its style but thought
itself, its shifts, its evasions, its magical ability to function
in many contexts at once—
it was the rock star—nerves jangling—veins open—who could tell *him*
anything?
the news/
paper
which had been folded over flat on the ground
yes/
terday is now
wide open—
the wind reads it—
To say that a poem is "about" self-consciousness is not to say that it is *only* about self-consciousness. There may be poems which are "only" about poetry and maybe —— wrote some of them, but if so, that is an extremely limited
conception
of poetry
Self-consciousness
is by its very nature expansive, passionate, interested, anxious to discover
resonances
of itself
at large in the world—
this desperate obsessive need to *talk*—
I walk through the house alone this morning—Song—
—Dry island. —Embattled sky. —Voices of the sea. —Strange flowering.
To tell you the truth I enjoyed chasing after you. Perhaps we could do it a couple of times a month.
passing by—her hands in her pockets—
what are *your* hands
doing?
to be *one,* to be *only,* to be *lone*—
There was an electronic tuning test at the Bell System exhibit in Disneyland. By pressing buttons you could hear either a tone of fixed frequency or a tone whose frequency you could adjust, but not both at the same time. After you had matched the frequencies as closely as possible, the machine scored your performance. My wife, who is a musician, did much better than

I.

I sit in the car in the exact middle of the front seat. I hear the announcer's voice as a compact sound source dead ahead, midway between the two speakers. As I move to the right, the sound source at first becomes diffuse. As I move further right, all the sound clearly comes from the right-hand speaker—

[my wife speaks this paragraph. as she speaks the last lines she moves to the right, gestures, indicates herself, "the right-hand speaker"]

I have said that, if a sound reaches us with equal intensities from two sources, we hear all of it as coming from the nearer source if the difference in distance is about a foot or greater. to dabble here—to wander—
"i before e except after c" tested by the word "atheist"
like cutting a path through the jungle
with a bureaucrat

Tempête dans un bénitier, Le Souverain Pontife avecque Les évêques, les archevêques, Nous font un satané chantier.	}	Tempest in a holy-water basin The Pope with His bishops and his archbishops Make a devilish mess for us

They don't know what they're losing—
All these wretched priests—

Sans le latin sans le latin La messe nous emmerde	}	Without Latin without Latin The Mass is shitty—

jnds of frequency or intensity—
se change en eau de boudin—changes into black pudding water—
The precedence effect, the fact that a sound seems to come from the direction from which it reaches us first, is bad for stereo, but highly desirable in everyday life. When someone speaks to you in a hard-walled room, you hear all the sound as coming from his or her mouth *[speaker indicates mouth]*
even though much of the sound that reaches you has been
reflected
from the walls—
her power over me is (what is the word?) *silence*—
whistles arrow from whirlwind—rain through his heart—
say what I'm called
and who rouses & calms my
power!—
It is characteristic of the mass media that the figures in them are all absent, not there, can't be touched. This is also true of books, which were in a sense the first of the mass media. Speaking to G.P. Skratz, I extended this idea to the Catholic "Mass" as well. The Mass is still another "mass" medium, an attempt to reach as many people as possible. At the beginning of the Mass, Christ is (and remains) profoundly absent, has not returned—and the Mass is, precisely, a fictional assertion that this is not the case, that Christ is in fact "present." ("Faith" = "the evidence of things *not seen*, the substance of things *hoped for*." Fiction!)
-the possibility that her disastrous relationships with men arise out of the desire to *prove her mother right*. "Men are such beasts—"
Too bad you didn't come with us to the restaurant. We found it (with a little trouble) & had just been seated when suddenly in pops Ishmael & Callahan & Alta & everybody so we all sat down together & ate too much Italian food & had a very nice time

What crazy birds
those crows who saw cut slice
the sound & good old branch
of the cross where they have perched
The name Cohan still has magic. The mere mention of it was enough to unleash a stream of talk from the two of them.
allied w/ leaves—soft-spoken—"Bend all your bows," said Robin Hood
"this day at the kirk of Gamry"
a sudden spasm—monstrous wings—
can't walk—can't talk—*furioso*—spasm—
EVIL IS EVERYWHERE TO BE
SEEN THERE IS NO
REST FROM IT
THE POWER OF DEATH
MULTIPLIES
THERE IS NO
"LIFE"—
And just when I might have reproached myself—It was Lucienne's thoughts, her mental attitudes, the plenitude of her being which I encountered. Not one of my kisses went astray.
estranged from that—much can be said—differently—
All these are promises made at a certain time (yet broken) to Love, which stands, wavering in a doorway, speaking words which I can neither hear nor—
love,
you are endless, sorrowful—
everything
in nature became fragmented before him—
"Gae hame, gae hame, good brother John, An tell your sister Sarah"
"she found him *drowned* in Yarrow"
fuck *you,* man to think of this again: think: forty years ago—
there: my face in the mirror—
the "hermeneutical situation"—
for "the letter killeth but the spirit"—the breath—
as the wind turns them (leaves)
they seem to say
"good-bye"—
soil—
bridge—
stone—
"Auld Ireland is calling"
Thousands of Madrid residents protested President Reagan's visit to Spain last night by banging on pots and pans and turning off their house lights—
I tied my drum to the top of my lance—
farewell
farewell
my sweet my
g'bye, love,
dark one, daughter— endlessly
blond dark fair sweet bitter mild soft harsh fiery

articulation of sound—
memory in the
"ear"—
a substitution

What crazy birds
those crows who saw cut slice
the sound & good old branch
of the cross where they have perched
The name Cohan still has magic. The mere mention of it was enough to unleash a stream of talk from the two of them.

[beginning here, the two voices—the two presences—speak simultaneously: the passage beginning, "allied with leaves" and ending, "soft harsh fiery" is spoken at the same time as the passage beginning, "—It might have been docks," and ending, "I pass by"]

—It might have been docks, it might have been blocks
It might have been—surely—the school of hard knocks
She might have detested all grandfather clocks
Or declared that she never could *bear* to wear frocks
But crossing her leotards (she didn't wear socks)
And squinting her eyes till she looked like a fox
(Ignoring my comment on bagels and lox)
She whispered obliquely, *The subject is rocks.*

We sat in the coffee house breathing the air
To the casual observer we hadn't a care
(It was Cambridge in Spring if you've ever been there)
When fixing upon me her vacuous stare
And assuming an attitude "born of despair"
She rather ungracefully fell from her chair
(The clamor they tell me resounded for *blocks!)*
And whispered obliquely, *The subject is rocks.*

And now that I'm older and very well read
It often occurs when I'm going to bed
That I wonder what *could* she have meant when she said
In a voice that might easily waken the dead
In a tone that was hollow and heavy as lead
With a tremor that filled me with Infinite Dread
(There were *so* many things she might speak of instead!)
But she grasped at a bundle of freshly picked phlox
And whispered obliquely, *The subject is rocks.*

East Oakland's Eastmont Mall. Eleven p.m., papers strewn everywhere. As I drive by the liquor store in my car I notice two men who seem to be confronting each other. One of them stands in front of the open liquor store. In his hands he holds an enormous rifle. The other is seated on a motorcycle. He is driving the motorcycle (as violently as he can) in small circles before the man with the rifle. Everything seems violent, open, uncertain. I pass by—

articulation of sound—
memory in the
"ear"—
a substitution

of the
"audible"
for
the
"visible"—

to write this day
to insist
upon it—

of the
"audible"
for
the
"visible"—

to write this day
to insist
upon it—

CHORUS: DARKNESS, THE LIGHT COMES SLOWLY

written for Richard Segasture's play, *Limbo*

Darkness. The light comes slowly.

What is it?
It sweetens the circulation of the blood.
My blood is circular enough already.
And your reasoning?
What is it?
Voices. Voices.

Up to now our considerations have been referred to a particular body of reference, which we have styled a "railway embankment." We suppose a very long train travelling along the rails with the constant velocity *v*

As far as I am able to judge, after long attending to the subject, the conditions of life appear to act in two ways: one

we see indefinite variability
out of millions of individuals
whether extremely slight
fact of this system?
to tame an animal
fed on nearly?
deviations of structure

what you call "ecstasy"
other people call
"rock
and
roll"

These are the
manifestations
of the real

Other relations between the species of enormous greenery

Manifestations of the
real
Movements in the
Sweetens the circulation of the blood

And your reasoning?
What is it?

They inculcated modesty as the great ornament of a woman and implicit reverence for her husband, softening their admonitions by such endearing admonitions as showed the fullness of a parent's love.

In the last rays of the sun, she
woke
thinking of nothing but

long black hair, covered in some parts of the country, by a veil made of a fine web, flowers, precious stones, and pearls from the Gulf of California

they are powerful enough
hybrid, and alone
but the faithless
a furious storm encountered

I was not now received as a stranger.

Said shee: I have never made my appearance out of Sweden. Everybody is so kind to me in my native land, but should I appear in Copenhagen and be hissed—! So I calmed her and said: Only a moderate voice and a little knowledge of acting will be successful. I believed she might safely venture.

but the storm came, for many days, the
vessel was tossed about, and all on board
were filled with apprehension, and no little
indignation
against the authors
of their calamities

ARE TWO EVENTS WHICH ARE SIMULTANEOUS WITH REFERENCE TO THE RAILWAY EMBANKMENT ALSO SIMULTANEOUS WITH REFERENCE TO THE TRAIN? WE SHALL SHOW DIRECTLY THAT THE ANSWER MUST BE IN THE NEGATIVE. AS A NATURAL CONSEQUENCE, THE FOLLOWING QUESTION ARISES:

(*there* is a phenomenon)

THE SKELETON'S DEFENSE OF CARNALITY!

Truly I have lost weight, I *have*
lost weight,
grown lean in love's defense,
in love's defense grown grave.
It was concupiscence
that brought me to the state:
all bone and a bit of skin
to keep the bone within.

Flesh is no heavy burden
for one possessed of little
and accustomed to its loss.
I lean to love, which leaves me lean
till lean turn into lack.

A wanton bone, I sing my song
and travel where the bone is blown
and extricate true love from lust
as any man of wisdom must.

Then wherefore should I rage
against this pilgrimage
from gravel unto gravel?
Circuitous I travel
from love to lack
and lack to lack,
from lean to lack
and back.

Darkness again. And into the play.

PROSE FOR TWO VOICES

Though I sleep as much as anyone else,
I am an advocate of being awake.

It had, he thought, a totemic resonance, that image of the woman suf-
It had, he thought, a totemic resonance, that image
fering. (This happened later, before I could.) In the dark I thought of
of the woman suffering. (This happened later, before I could.)
her. How can you say that she asked. How can you say that. Undulate,
In the dark I thought of her. How can you say that she asked.
fish. I spoke to her for about fifteen minutes. This is the guarded situ-
How can you say that. Undulate, fish. I spoke to her for about
ation. I am in my thoughts. This is a recollection of last night when we
fifteen minutes. This is the guarded situation. I am in my
all saw a film. I wanted. Children sound and resound. The image of a
thoughts. This is a recollection of last night when we all saw
house, filled with happy children. What more than that. We'll all be in
a film. I wanted. Children sound and resound. The image of a
that house he promised. We'll all be happy. Night darkens. Stains. I am
house, filled with happy children. What more than that. We'll all
in the dream of the happy woman. Terrific! she said. As she crossed her
be in that house he promised. We'll all be happy. Night darkens.
legs I thought: *The Renaissance.* Her lipstick turned her mouth into a
Stains. I am in the dream of the happy woman. Terrific she said.
scar. I adored him I adored him. Come. Now. I want to play ball. I
As she crossed her legs I thought: The Renaissance. *Her lipstick*
want you to tell me how I can do it. I don't know. Whenever he opens his
turns her mouth into a scar. I adored him I adored him. Come. Now.
mouth something happens. She was alone so she took off her dress. Now I
I want to play ball. I want you to tell me how I can do it. I don't
am closing the door. I am opening the transit. Folie de doute. What a
know. Whenever he opens his mouth something happens. She was alone
word! I saw you, don't deny it. She had (or so I thought) a totemic reso-
so she took off her dress. Now I am closing the door. I am opening
nance, that image of the tall woman suffering.

the transit. Folie de doute. What a word! I saw you, don't deny it.
She had (or so I thought) a totemic resonance, that image
of the tall woman
suffering

from TURNING FORTY

which Lucienne would I seek to seize and know again? The naked amorous one flushed with ardour? Or the friend, the comrade, she who walked by my side through the long streets? And more simply still, Lucienne, the creature who bore that name, never seen elsewhere, irreplaceable? What would be most important then: the memory of having possessed her or the assurance of faithfully owning some earnest, some inimitable signature, as though an imprint of our tiny being on common space (that harsh space identical in substance with separation and with death)? Yes, to see again in all its precision the act of smoothing the hair, or flicking a dress to smooth out the folds (merely to think of that is to want to weep aloud) —Jules Romains, *The Body's Rapture*

BUS RIDE
His father was of a cheerful disposition, his mother of a quite melancholy temper; both contributed to the character of the child. Do you have the time, she said. He was standing almost rooted to the spot waiting for a bus. Some are quick to notice, others require convalescence. She was not speaking to him. The bus had not arrived. I have hoped for some time, he thought, to have entered into an agreement with certain people, but the substance has rarely shown itself in ingenuity and depth. Her unmistakable body entered the bus. The light was changing slowly all around him. He stood. I have hoped for some time, he thought, to have achieved a modus operandi. Now he felt the slight chill which was the mark of the beginning of the evening. But I have failed in this. It was as if he were attempting to turn to stone. Do you know what time the next bus is she said. He stood. She did not repeat her question. The bus, his bus, had not yet arrived. He could feel her eyes on him. He stood there, rooted, like a tree. There was a tree behind him. He had no idea what sort of tree. Sometimes, at the beginning of a story, you can sense what it was that made the writer begin that story. The beginning is always interesting. The light had changed, perceptibly. He wondered if she would repeat her question. Diphtheria. Someone was standing behind him. Each night he had stayed home hoping to have achieved some understanding. He watched carefully now, carefully. He entered the bus. No one was getting out.

After a long convalescence of three years or more he had returned to the grammar school. His word box had increased perceptibly.

SHAKESPEARE

CAMBRIDGE SELECTION

Inside there was a picture of a man and a book. Sometimes in a story one can follow the twists and turnings of an author's mind. The bus was moving in an unfamiliar landscape. He would have to go downtown. But the landscape, here, was unfamiliar. He watched as it passed by, slowly. The bus turned. It stopped. What do you think of a person in a particular way that is time, he thought. She was smiling at him but not directly. What do you think of a person who is almost forty years old and still unable to tie his shoelaces. That's what he is. Almost forty years old and still unable to tie his shoelaces. His mother has to do it for him.

She was sitting directly across from him but she had not spoken. The two women who had been speaking stopped. He wondered if there had been something he should have said. She arose and rang the bell. *As the landscape changed it became more like something he remembered.* As a result of a great mischance he had grown up with a melancholy and irritable temperament such as belongs to men of ingenuity and depth; thanks to the one, they are quick as lightning in perception, thanks to the other, they take no pleasure in verbal cleverness or falsehood. As the landscape changed it became like something he remembered. His mother stood over him wondering what to say. He said, I don't want you to do that again. It was time. The bus stopped. Longing for the release the story promises, the writer begins. I have never done that to you she said. Not ever. *I have never yet broken your skin when I hit you with my fists.*

To which my Lord responded:

That though for his part he cared not whether there were witches or no; yet his opinion was: That the Confession of Witches, and their sufferings for it proceeded from an erroneous belief, viz, That they had made a contract with the Devil to serve him for such Rewards as were in his power to give them; and that it was their Religion to worship and adore him; in which Religion they had such firm and constant belief, that if anything came to pass according to their desire, they believed the Devil had heard their prayers, and granted their requests, for which they gave him thanks; but if things fell out contrary to their prayers and desires, then they were troubled at it, fearing that they had offended him, and not served him as they ought, and asked him for forgiveness of their offences. Also (said my Lord) they imagine their dreams are real exterior actions...

I leave it to you, O Nut of Knowledge
The Girls at home and the Boys in college

"Promise me that you won't do it."
So
I promised her.
But

I did it.
Rip cord of the sky's acetylene.
It was a raft of purposes, who could have told what came of it

After the night, expenditure
at the high
what clouds this morning
who could have said—

you
are neither Substance nor Shadow

The roar of Thor Gadwa's chainsaw shattered the spooky silence of the ashen-gray wilderness around him yesterday. *Rip cord of the sky's acetylene.*

Good morning, Carolyn! *Rip cord of the sky's acetylene* What are you doing up so early? *Great blue* I've got to be out of here by seven! *All* We're taking a group of our special ed kids out to the island on a field trip! *Out of proportion* You like your work don't you? *It was a raft of purposes who could have said what came of it* It can be the most frustrating—but also the most rewarding when you see the results you can get with slow learners *Rip cord, rip cord of the sky's acetylene*

There is a certain kind of light which can be seen only at certain times of day. I had tried to find it then but was not able. There is a certain hint of dusk as well which can be seen at times though rarely written of or praised. I had hoped to see you. Afterwards it was necessary to begin, again and again.

Dearest, neither you nor I in this late sun can be seen more clearly.

In Crete there was the procession of the Sacred Heart

He was a boy of high spirits and impatient of rest; but at the age of seven he fell head first from the top of a ladder to the floor below, and remained a good five hours without motion or consciousness. The right side of the cranium was fractured, but the skin was not broken. The fracture gave rise to a large tumor, and the child suffered much loss of blood from the many deep lancings. The surgeon, indeed, observing the broken cranium and considering the long period of unconsciousness, predicted that he would either die of it or grow up an idiot. However by God's grace neither part of his prediction came true, but as a result of this mischance he grew up with a melancholy and irritable temperament such as belongs to men of ingenuity and depth, who, thanks to the one, are quick as lightning in perception, and thanks to the other, take no pleasure in verbal cleverness or falsehood.

From flock and from down to rise—

Take it to heart!—were folly for thee

This is the oppressor. This is the oppressor's language. The wind, the wind cut short the speech of George Bush to a GOP delegation at the Hilton Inn near the Detroit Metropolitan Airport, yesterday, at four o'clock, here, in the capital of Hatred and Bitterness!

Dignity and Good Luck be yours

After biting the mouth merges with her skin

Flock upon flock—up
in the sky

one feels that he would have agreed with the Duke of Newcastle who, in his discourse with Hobbes, affirms in the clearest fashion his belief in the religion of witchcraft as a fact

'contrarie' rites and ceremonies

look, at the first rift of the sky he
turned his head and
severed his attention   clouds
rammed into clouds   the dark

and com and daunce with me
in Irlonde

"Faggot, I burn thee"

Love speaks, barely, in this century. He kissed her hard upon the mouth, thrusting his tongue inside. Her hands were caressing his ass then pressing his cock against her cunt. Uh.

They are images of longing, she said. Often sexual. They were walking, quickly, away from the building. She spoke without design, spontaneously.

Her hard eyes followed him along the corridor. Darkness

having in the name of the Holy Trinity, sprinkled a little water, quelled the waves

I shall go into a hare

With sorrow and sighing and mickle care

I am become a transparent eyeball; I am nothing; I see all

This
is the ship I am
building
It is
a ship of death yes
Harvest. Darkness. They
split the air with their cries   Love

There is nothing self-contradictory in the thought of many actual entities with the same abstract essence, apart from the reiteration gained from never societies. In proportion to the choas there is triviality. There are different types of order; and it is not ttrue that in proportion to the orderliness there is depth. There are vari us types of order, and some of them provide more trivial satisfaction than do others. Thus, if there is to be progress beyond limited ideals, the course of history by way of escape must venture along the borders of chaos in its substitution of higher for lower types of order.

Speak, animal,
ere I be brought to ground

The depression
in your voice stays with me
What to do when there is something
always hanging over your
head "And the weather is cold."
Dockside, the boat is moving
How to express anything
Look, there is a possibility over there on that far
island, and a tree, which,
once gazed upon, can barely be
forgotten. Leaves fall, even in California.
How do we look when once those eyes
which others praise more finely still than
I
cease looking, and the word "change"
and the word "kill" and the word "cold"
come close, and your voice,
which was only a projection of the
telephone,
                    comes close:

FIFTY

The Irish language
is alive and
thriving
in a former flax mill
in West Belfast.

Alone.
1-2-3-
Anything for You.

Prosecutor Jon Goodfellow is seeking
a first-degree murder conviction and a finding
of special circumstance of murder during
the commission of a robbery, which could
result in the death penalty for Turner.
But (said Ennix)
Turner killed Washington
in the heat of passion.

newspaper article:
The Tribune
3/28/90

"The first blow of the hunter's steel
Caused the poor girl's mind to reel
'Hunter, dear Hunter, what have you done?'"

on edge, waiting for Grifo to arrive, he's late,

I may be misrepresenting the depth of your feelings towards me. But sepa-
ration
should make that clearer. We need to clarify

Blue Bayou
Cryin'
Desperado
Lock Stock & Teardrops

We have come a long way (Magi)

from what we felt
only a short time ago

possibility at any rate
sleeping with Dan
and this has coincided with your

You must let me be
"exploratory"

Love Is A Rose
San Antonio Rose
Pink/Cadillac

she thought maybe the problem was she hadn't slept with him so she did that
she said sleeping with him was
"exploratory"

You Ought To Be Here With Me
Be A Lion
Ooh, Baby, Baby

these are
solemnities
of light!

this stupendous increase in mass!
whenever he attempts to "locate" it
the spiritual has now retired from the "outer"
connected to the experience of *cities*
spectator's process of association (here) in view of these changes

read, & was chilled (call me "Johnny Church")

At the Hop At the Hop
the fiction of the innocence & purity of the adolescent self

what she told me she *did* / ran counter / to what she told me / she *felt*

your presence
floods in upon me

It's So Easy
Long, Long Time (you're a fuckin *queen*)
Teardrops

The greatest gift of a garden is the restoration of the five senses.

Everyone knows to what an extent women are afflicted with nervous disorders.

During these years—both of us working at home, both of us sharing in chores (cooking, cleaning, splitting wood, canning, sewing)—we also raised three children.

Betty & I were married in 1919 and came to live in Edgartown, Mass.

The first strawberry shrub I ever saw was given to me as a small child by a red-cheeked boy just as I went into church with my grandmother.

Jerusalem Artichoke, Earth Apple, Canada Potato, Girasole, Wild Sunflower—
has an interesting history similar to the dark-centered common /
"garden"
"sunflower"

In a musty old tome printed in 1649 and entitled "A Perfect Description of Virginia" we read that—

After many gardens have been considered (and their inhabitants located and scanned) it often seems that those in which the "individuality" of the owners had run riot are the ones to live longest in the memory

but failed utterly in *permanent* influence

OLD WOMEN AFFECT CLOVER
The speaker argued that old women kept cats; cats killed mice; mice were prone to destroy the nests of the bumble-bees, which alone were fitted, owing to the length of their proboscises, to fertilize the blossoms of the clover. Consequently, a good supply of clover depended on an abundance of old women.

To many of us, said Dr. Holmes, the unique aroma of the
Box,
cleanly bitter
in scent as in taste, is redolent of the
"Eternal Past"—

I find Sweet Peas can hardly have too rich a soil, provided always that they are kept sufficiently wet. They *must* have moisture...

Flowers are the expression of God's love to man.

—That image came straight out of my unconscious.
—Your unconscious draws like Picasso.

It is now ten years since we put in our garden: four hundred trees, several hundred paintings, four books, and three children later.

are drifting apart—she has been very "busy"

What she wants, she sd, is in-
                    timacy, what she'll settle for is Power—

Children! she said bitterly, CHILDREN HAVE NO MEMORY!

Magick
Tracks of My Tears
I'll Always Love You

frame piece *never* blood arch blood bone semen oil

meeting *him* I remembered very well how I had loved *you*   Time!
                    (after all these years)

I came to call Betsey the "rabbi of the trees"

Judy Grahn, yesterday, seeing my mother's photograph: "She was beautiful." I said (& thought): "Yes, she was."

fearful
fearful of intimacy
she lay back—
Sweetness—

This is Jack Foley
and Benjamin Lindgren
telling you about a KPFA Marathon special

Kundalini, climb, bend, as it were,

this power *upward,*

What is it like to be a poet at this moment in the United States? To what extremities & myths are we driven?

When Will I Be Loved?
You Took Advantage of Me
You're No Good

she is at the *edge*
of everything

J'ai appris hier...
Violence du langage, extreme intensité des cris, apparente incohérence de l'ensemble!

The split between the claims put forth in the introduction and the actual accomplishment of the verse might profitably be compared to

THE GRAND CANYON

—Never confuse effort with results!
—Never confuse clichés with remarks!

The paradoxical state of the mind itself—its limited/unlimited nature, its ability to consider absolutely anything under the sun—what Jake calls its source in the "everywhere"—matched against the limitations *everything in the world places on it.*

I hear them in the folds of air.

look
at the way
that woman's
dress
folds
as she sits,
revealing
but concealing
the curve
of her
breasts—
(Presence in Absence)—

It was an
"Innocence of the Flesh"—
an awareness
that Desire itself
was
Innocent!—

She's only spoken twice, and both times she said: "Dr. Rex Morgan!"

a mien of surface decorum masking a mind on the verge of chaos, about to snap, a world of quiet comic desperation where nothing works the way it's supposed to and everything is about to fly apart

speaking with you was like making contact with a side of civilization I am not used to here in New York where suspicion seems to rule and kindness is an exception—

speech-based poetry
which tends to be rooted in what can be spoken only
in
the
"neighborhood"

She phoned me on Friday to tell me she loved me.
a speech-based poetry
"Don't worry, the car can find its own way."

I hear them in the folds of air. We both get out. She says, "Don't worry, the car can find its own way."

Earthquake. Tuesday, 10/17/89, 5:04 p.m.

The second time only I came.

I was less present, she said, *I have begun to break away from you.*

any individual word, any part of the languages which were scattered with the fall of Babel, contains within itself the potentiality of returning to its source: once awakened into life, any word may, through its infinite connections with other words, its "inflexions and movements," return us to the divine. The poet "listens" to the Logos; the poem is "dictated"

she wanted *me* to feel that pain

I want to be independent of you
You *are* independent of me
I want to be independent of you
You *are* independent of me

In *The Cult of The Black Virgin*—a book I read with
considerable interest and would recommend to others—
Ean Begg writes of Pope Sylvester II (*c.* 940-1003):

Although this unorthodox and Gnosticizing Pope exuded
the odour of sanctity from his incorrupt body, he was
never raised to the altars of the Church. The first
Frenchman to be Pope, he acceded to the throne of
Peter in 999, fortunate inversion of 666, the number
of the Great Beast, at a time when the world was
awaiting the dreaded millennium. According to one
legend, he seduced the daughter of his alchemist master
in order to learn the secret of secrets and was expelled
from Spain. In another version he met a maiden
of marvellous beauty, brilliant in gold and tissues of silk,
who told him her name was Meridiana ("the lady of the south")
and who offered him her body, her riches and her magical
wisdom if he would trust her. Gerbert agreed to the
bargain and in a short time became successively Archbishop
of Rheims, where Clovis was anointed, Archbishop of
Ravenna, where Mérovée spent his youth, and Pope.
As well as being the first Christian alchemist, credited
with achieving the great work, he also had a talking head,
which seems to have operated like a primitive computer.
He introduced Arabic numbers to the West and invented the
clock, the astrolabe and the hydraulic organ. In the realm
of politics, he attempted to raise a crusade for the
liberation of the Holy Land and established the Church in
Hungary, ancient Sicambria, making Stephen its...king.

a review

(1986, Routledge and Kegan Paul Inc., $11.95)

a woman about my age, bored, on the street—
suddenly her eyes look up

she loved me for the space of a demisemiquaver

I was in the 3rd from right lane—pouring rain!
car in front of me hits brakes
I do also but they don't seem to take
I'm heading straight for him—skidding
I turn the wheel to the left, cross over the left lane,
  & hit the dividing wall with the left front end of the car.
Stop.

[a true incident but a metaphor for the poem itself]

a speech-sourced poetry

folds
as she sits
revealing
but concealing
the curve
of her
body

my stupe-
          stupe-
he said: Forgive my stupefaction!—

WE HAVE HERE—AS WE HAVE AT THE CONCLUSION OF "THE ECHOING GREEN"—A KIND OF GRADUAL FADING OF THE LIGHT IN WHICH THINGS ARE NO LONGER SEEN CLEARLY AND IN WHICH THE SOUNDS WE "HEAR" TEND TO BECOME SOMEWHAT DISTANT: "ALL THE HILLS ECHOED." AT THIS POINT, I THINK, LANGUAGE BECOMES SOMETHING CLOSE TO PURE POTENTIALITY, TO PURE "SOUND" OR "MUSIC," TO THE "SONG" THAT THE PIPER PIPES. WHAT BLAKE IS ATTEMPTING TO MAKE US DO, I SUSPECT, IS TO TREAT *ALL* OF HIS WORDS IN THE SAME WAY THAT WE MUST TREAT THE NAMES OF HIS CHARACTERS: WE MUST CONTINUALLY RECOMBINE THEM, MUST TURN THEM AROUND AND AROUND IN OUR MINDS UNTIL THEY BECOME WORDS WHICH, THOUGH DIFFERENT, INVOLVING OTHER LETTERS, RETAIN IN THEIR SOUNDS THE ECHOES OF ONE ANOTHER. BLAKE HIMSELF USED WORDS OF THE BIBLE IN ORDER TO CREATE NEW HARMONIES, HARMONIES WHICH "CHIMED" WITH THOSE OF THE BIBLE, AND I THINK "HOLY THURSDAY" WAS MEANT TO SERVE THE SAME PURPOSE. TWAS ON A, FOR EXAMPLE, MIGHT EASILY BECOME TWAS HONOR, HOSANNA; THE SEATS OF HEAVEN, THE SAINTS OF HEAVEN, THE SEEDS OF HEAVEN; BENEATH THEM SIT, BE NEATH THEM SAID; WHITE AS SNOW, WHY 'TIS SNOW, WHY 'TIS NOW; TILL INTO, TELL UNTO, TOLL UNTO; THE VOICE OF SONG, THEY VOICE HIS SONG, THEIR VOICE IS SONG, THEIR VOICE, HIS SONG; THE FLOWERS OF LONDON TOWN, OR LAND ATONED, OR LENTEN TIME; BUT MULTITUDES OF LAMBS, BUT MULTITUDES OF

LANDS, BUT MULTITUDES OF LIMBS, BOUGHT MULTITUDES OF LAMBS; THOUSANDS OF LITTLE BOYS, THOSE SANDS OF LITTLE BOYS; O WHAT A, O WATER; THE HUM OF MULTITUDES, THE HOME OF MULTITUDES, THE HYMN, THE HAM, THE HIM OF MULTITUDES; THEY LIKE THAMES WATERS FLOW, THEY LIGHT TIME'S WATERS FLOW, THEIR NIGHTTIMES WATERS FLOW; RADIANCE ALL THEIR OWN, RADIANCE ALL THEREROUND, RADIANCE ALL THEREON, REGENTS ARE THERE CROWNED; THE CHILDREN WALKING, THE CAULDRON WAKING, THE CALLED ARE WALKING; HARMONIOUS THUNDERINGS, OUR MOAN, HIS THUNDERINGS; THE VOICE, THE VOWS, THE JOYS.

—Not before or since. This woman had the secret!

Lady Meryon, with her escort of girls and subalterns, came daintily past the hotel compound and startled me from my brooding with her pretty silvery voice. "Dreaming, Mr. Clifden? It isn't at all wholesome to dream in the East! Come and dine with us tomorrow. A tiny dance afterwards, or Bridge for those who like it."

had an orgasm with him but wasn't quite present
told me she planned to have sex casually, "as a *man* has sex"—

"It's you I love"   Beauty!—

I'm uncertain of your life. It frightens me.

She sighed. Was it for the lost dance or for the lost soldier lying out on the barren hills in the tremendously dying sunset?

not to see each other for a while. You may find you miss me. You may find you don't.

thundering horses!—

"Life"—

You say one kind of thing to me, another kind of thing to him. You need to clarify, clarify—

Dear Heart!

I think that love is a Freudian slip. I think it's a necessary experiment. I think I don't need to revise a whole lot. I think there must be something to what he says. I think there must be something to what he thinks. I own your comb. How are your teeth doing these days? I think you're the most wonderful person I—

dreamlife

And in grace and elegance of manners, in skill in the arts of Poetry and the Lute, who could surpass them?

fungus and a dish of slugs entrapped

here, she said, listening to him intently, here, here is my heart!

At 50
a testament—

Still, once upon a time, at the beginning of Western thought,—
the essence of language "flashed" in the light of Being!

"Ethnic" utterances presuppose a *context* out of which they arise. They are never statements of an "isolated ego." This, she sd, is the point at which *genetic* inheritance becomes *cultural* inheritance.

After Flossie and William Carlos Williams had ended their interview with James Joyce, they left the apartment. The renowned author referred to them later as "beati innocenti," blessed innocents, innocents abroad. *This story is misremembered.* It was himself and Nora that Joyce referred to as "beati innocenti"! (*Where are the innocents we slaughter?)*

"immature"

"relationship"

What is it, dearest?—dissolution?—yes—
the face I had, you see, will come a
gain, yes,
she—

(a woman, dead at 55)

it is time to make a will. What piece of fruit to eat?

The family, music, harmony, dissonance—all seem to move together in this highly "sounded" piece, turning "grief"—some family quarrel probably (SHE GIVES ME NOTHING BUT GRIEF)—to "music"

silence— susurration—
Don't listen to him—he's just my televersion!

"I would leave, not a record of something realized...but..."

how can we / speak of the
"heart"?

what possibilities of
"tenderness"

In her bleeding, she insists on my presence at all times. (She is afraid)

Larry says the last word of his poem must be *past.* I suggested, since it was p-a-s-y, it could also be *easy.* But he pointed out that the y and the t were next to each other on the typewriter and so *that* typo was more likely.

My favorites are PARABOLA: MYTH & THE QUEST FOR MEANING, RARITAN QUARTERLY, and BOMB MAGAZINE—though that last should perhaps be BOMB *A* MAGAZINE

These are the signs of a failing relationship!

You might be asking, "Why are people consulting me about property values?" You inspire confidence, many seek reassurance by being with you, obtaining guidance. You exude qualities of mysticism, intellect.

The world is damned

—in the crowded
dept. store
hope
blossoms
in the
underwear
aisles—
leave out the vowels—like Hebrew—
Yr eyes
search me out—
they want to have a

"relationship" a
"relationship" don't they?
High above,
clouds lour—
fragments—
as the mind?
moves *around* objects, not into them
or else
centers in NOTHING
this dept.
store this
crowd:
nothing
Forgive me,
them—
people
pass & smile
clouds,
like
mind—
meditative
but not ecstatic
mind awake
but not
intensely so—
"born to shop"
the poem a
response
to the boredom
& the weight
of
bodies
which is
what I feel
as these
strangers
walk about me
"These pants are WET!"—
I
close my eyes
to
SLEEP

(gesture: indicates
audience: "strangers")

THE TIGER

to the memory of my friend, Michael Lurie

There is a constant play of light and color on the bellying square sails (silver in moonlight, black in starlight, cloth-of-gold at sunset, white as the clouds themselves at noon)— [S.E. Morison, *Christopher Columbus, Mariner*]

He was about twelve years old. Born in East Oakland. Black. Dark-brown in color. He stared for a long time at a wall in San Francisco on which was written the words, FUCK NIGGERS. Why couldn't any of us say anything about it? One of us said (later), "I realized at that time how much of a 'womb' East Oakland was."

the failure to attack it
to attack racism
whenever and wherever it
occurs—

She did not wish to create a "character" or to find a "place" for that character to live. She wished to release something. Yet there were so many contrary currents within her that the release of one called to mind all the others which had *not* been released. The alternative was silence, but of course she wanted anything but silence. It was in the midst of this quandary that she encountered... (a constant play of light and color)

On the morning after Raguk had seen sixteen tigers leaping from the sky he awoke feeling strangely uneasy. He had of course assumed that it was a dream or an hallucination. But the tigers had been real enough. They had probably originated on Og's second moon—or so he thought as he gazed, rather stupidly as usual, up into the night sky on this one clear night in the month of Mar. One, two, three...sixteen leaping from the moon down to his own land of Ur. He had heard of such things in the ancient prophecies—*blood moon tiger child*—but he had no idea what they could have meant. Why should they suddenly appear—and why to him, a poor mekam driver? Still, how beautiful they were—leaping one after another, shimmering in that dreamlight, powerful, throbbing with all the energy of life...

"Raguk...Raguk...why are you up?"

It was his wife, Dar.

"To see the most glorious sight I have ever seen. Look."

Dar gave a slight gasp as she saw them too. One after another—glorious animals!

"Why, they're beautiful," she said. "But whyever should they come here? This—this is nowhere."

"Perhaps they have come to bring us some good," said Raguk.

"What possible good could they bring?" said Dar, continuing to stare.

Now, at that moment a very odd thing happened to them, and it happened to both Raguk and Dar at the same time. They were both aware—it was not a voice but an awareness, like the sudden instantaneous solution to a problem in mathematics—of a vast benevolence which encompassed everything around them, birds trees flowers rocks sky, even themselves, the poor human creatures. It was a cry of REJOICE suddenly leaping up from the heart of things, a wild and ecstatic *clarification* of consciousness. Raguk, who understood very little of his life and who was pained by his knowledge of understanding very little, involuntarily smiled and began to sing a song he had never heard before.

"Lagoolee, lagoolee, esthur, esthur..."

He had a very bad voice and little ear for music but somehow the tune was haunting all the same.

"Rocks, barrenness," said Dar, "song is springing forth out of the barren soil. It is a miracle, Raguk."

And then—quite suddenly—there was no miracle. The tigers disappeared. Nothing was left of them, no tracks, sounds, nothing. Nothing was left but the continuous red sheen of Og's second moon.

"Raguk...where could they have gone?"

"I—don't know."

Raguk raised his hand to his brow and looked out over that night landscape. Nothing was there. Only a few shadows—rocks, boulders. But nothing alive, nothing breathing. The landscape was dead again.

"Raguk—shouldn't we...examine? Search?"

And search they did. Raguk lighted his mogore lamp and held it above his head as he scrambled among the lifeless things that stretched out for miles around his house. Nothing. Still nothing.

"Come," said Dar at last. "Come. Perhaps some sleep will help."

And so they tried to sleep. In his dreams Raguk attempted to see the creatures again but they had ceased to appear even to his dreams. He could remember nothing but the extraordinary fact of the event itself.

In the morning he awoke and felt—uneasy.

"Dar, did we—could we—"

"I don't know, Raguk."

"Dar, we must tell no one of this."

"No. Yes. No one, Raguk."

"Not even Dareena."

"Especially Dareena."

"We must think, Dar."

"Yes, Raguk. We must *think.*"

But no matter how much they thought—or how hard they thought—they discovered: nothing.

Sun-flash on the pool. My son Sean, 9, holds his head under the water to the count of six, then ten. Kicking is next. Sean in blue bathing cap, the little "black" girl next to him in red. In the crowded pool bodies "rearrange" themselves. What good is a book (she said) if no one will read it?

all of our presidents
from Kennedy on
have been failures!
on the loud hill
the wind
whips up from the miles
away!
looking at our country
is like looking at a map
of schizophrenia!—
streaks of cloud that frame the blue—

Imagine: a fat man a very fat man waddling along in what must seem to your eyes a soiled blue sheet. This is Urik, chief priest of our village. I had always avoided him even though, like everyone else, I was required to attend his services once a week. A short fat darkskinned man (I am a tall thin darkskinned man) waddling through the marketplace where I stood attending to my mekam. Sire Urik, said the ignorant populace, touch me, Sire Urik. Sire Urik, heal my disease. Even the young women: Touch me, Sire Urik. How I hated him.

"Raguk."

The sound of my own name startled me. I had no idea that Urik knew me at all. He said it again:

"Raguk!"

After a pause I answered him. Obsequiousness. "Ah, yes, Sire Urik."

"You have seen the vision of the sixteen tigers."

"Wh-what?"

"You have seen the vision of the sixteen tigers. Do not deny it, I am certain of it anyway."

"How—how do you know, Sire Urik? Did Dar—"

"Not a word. I *know*, that's all." Urik's eyes blazed.

"But if you *know*, Sire Urik, you must know what the vision *means*. It has been an enormous burden to me. You must *tell* me, Sire Urik."

The blaze went out of his eyes.

"Unfortunately, I do not know *that*. There, unhappily, the prophecies are not clear."

"For the gods' sake, what prophecies, Sire Urik?"

"In the sixteenth chapter of the second Book of Reegam it is written that a puny and insignificant mekam driver will be granted the extraordinary vision of sixteen tigers leaping from the sky. And *then*—"

"And *then*—"

"And then, unfortunately, the text is corrupt. No one knows what 'and then' refers to."

"There are no opinions on the subject?"

"None. It is the most profoundly puzzling passage in all our scripture. Would you care to see it?"

"Of course."

"Come."

We made our way from the marketplace to the ancient temple which stood a mile away from the town. Urik signalled me to follow him inside. At the far corner of the dusty room stood an enormous bookcase. Urik sighed as he failed to reach a large blue book three shelves up. Finally he jumped into the air and pulled it down. In a moment the book was opened to the proper page. It was just as he had said. The passage began coherently enough but it ended in hopeless gibberish.

"Is there no one who can understand this?" I asked.

"No one," said Urik. "It is completely unintelligible. I was rather hoping that *you* would be able to tell *me*..."

Outside, night was beginning to fall. The red moon rose. I noticed a shaft of light pierce through the enormous windows which thrust their bulk upon every wall of the temple. I thought: The second moon is rising, covering everything with its blood.

"Urik, I can bear this no longer. I have begun to dream things."

"What things?"

"Fearful things. Dreadful. Also, things have begun to happen to me. Yesterday I fell down a flight of stairs. Only I didn't fall, something *tripped* me."

"You are being singled out."

"For what purpose?"

"I don't know. I can't tell you any more than that. You are being singled out. I don't know."

"I am not a handsome man, I am fifty years old I am cowardly and low I do not understand things as I ought I have no mission in life I am only a mekam driver (my father before me was a mekam driver his father before him was a mekam driver) I have no purpose. You must understand that nothing I have ever done or learned has in any way prepared me for this."

"None of that is relevant. You are being singled out. Do you remember Lackeem?"

"Lackeem?...Lackeem the idiot?"

"He was not an idiot. At the age of thirty-five his eyes began suddenly to cross. He tried every means at his disposal to drive them apart again. He focused one eye on one object, the other eye on another object, and then he would *move* the objects. Slowly, painfully, he would succeed in uncrossing his eyes. But the very next moment—wham!—back they were: crossed again."

"Lackeem was well known as the village idiot. Everyone thought of him as that."

"Lackeem was a saint."

"A saint? Urik, how am I to understand this? Do you remember how he drooled?"

"I used to talk to him nightly. He was on the whole less argumentative than you. He would sit upon the temple steps and say, 'Urik, I have been singled out. The gods'—but he had no idea *which* gods—'have visited me with a special affliction, I am among the chosen.'"

"And what did you say to him?"

"What could I say? I could not deny it. He had been chosen. I remember him on his death bed, his long hair filthy with many years of neglect, his body soiled by his own excrement. 'Urik,' he said to me, 'Urik, I have been chosen, I have been singled out.' Even in death his eyes were crossed. Remarkable!"

"But did he never *do* anything? Urik, he must have been chosen for some purpose."

"Not necessarily, though of course there were many aspects of him of which I was ignorant. I must say that I regarded myself as the learner in this situation. It is possible that his mission was to prepare the world for *you*."

"For *me*?"

"Yes, of course. Like you he was singled out. I knew it the moment I saw you that day in the marketplace. His image flashed into my mind and I thought, 'Raguk! Raguk has been chosen!'"

"But my eyes aren't crossed. I'm not the village idiot. I am a mekam driver. My father was a mekam driver. That is all I am. A mekam driver."

"You are a mekam driver who has seen a vision. I knew that too."

"But did Lackeem ever refer to this vision of the sixteen tigers?"

"Not in so many words, no."

"But can't you see that my case is therefore entirely different?"

"No, not necessarily. One must allow for some latitude in these matters. It may be that you have been chosen by a god *different* from the one who chose Lackeem."

"But by *which* different god?"

"I don't know."

"And for what purpose?"

"I don't know."

Jesse's graduation. My arm is situated uncomfortably on the second rail of a metal railing. Downstairs I see a basketball court on which rows of chairs have been neatly arranged. Children with rifles march out. They are wearing dark green uniforms with shining silver helmets. ROTC. The military here too. The school's colors are a mismatched green—brighter than the uniforms—and gold. The gold tends towards orange, thus mismatching. There is a large sign

FREMONT

in gold on a green cloth background. The graduates march in to "Gaudiamus, Igitur." The men are in green, the women in yellow. Several wave to the audience, are applauded. Their moment of public triumph... Jesse is seventeen years old and half black, half white. When he answers the telephone he intentionally lowers his voice.

Raguk begins to seek out other opinions. He examines texts. Learns languages. Consults experts.

"Have you found out anything?" asks Urik.

"No, nothing."

"Have you at least remembered those words you spoke?"

"No!"

Mightn't it be a public prophecy, having to do with the health of the land? Or perhaps political? Oughtn't the king to know of this?

And so Raguk is summoned before the king.

"You don't know the meaning of this sign?"

"I do not, your Majesty!"

"Doctors, come forth to examine this man."

They do so. At last one of them steps forward.

"As far as we can determine, your Majesty, he is a perfectly normal man. A little on the stupid side, perhaps. But perfectly normal."

Raguk, who has begun to become famous, is allowed to leave. Outside, on the palace grounds, a crowd has gathered to see him. Someone says: "Stick to your guns, Raguk." Another: "Good man, Raguk!" He acknowledges them by a wave of the hand.

Dar walks in the metal garden.

Rabbi Judah said: *Nefesh* and *ruah* are conjoined, while *neshamah* has its abode in the character of a man, which place remains unknown and undiscovered. If a man strive to a pure life, he is therein assisted by holy *neshamah,* through the which he is made pure and saintly and attains to the name of holy. But if he does not strive to be righteous and pure of life, there does not animate him holy *neshamah,* but only the two grades, *nefesh* and *ruah.* More than that, he who enters into impurity is led further into it, and he is deprived of heavenly aid. Thus, each is moved forward upon the way which he takes. [*Zohar,* ed. Gershom G. Scholem]

he spoke quickly, as if hoping to find some other excuse for reckoning, as if, in the stiff umbrage of his circumstance, he remained somehow hopeless, unnerved, smitten, without reserve or resonance, spiteful even to the wind, which, engaged in other business (roaring) in a plain treasure, spoke slowly, groping endlessly, funneled, wretched stuff of vixen, vision, heart of the whole, heart of two minds, matters/listen/I speak/in bro-
ken/sentences/un/able to/sift one/thought from/another/in/the dark,/really./I/
think of you and/words/hasten, break/
in the effort, break,—
shattering, the words go out—

Dar walks in the metal garden. Once it had been something to see. The aluminum marigolds catch the sun, like razors. The copper roses go on blossoming. Now...She remembers something. What was it, *who* was it? Her father? Someone's father? His name was Abel, Abe, Abraham, he had owned a book store, there was a sign on the door, Blake's *The Tyger,* an old story told her by someone, true? false?, Abraham walking home, reached his house, opened the door, someone there?—

"Reality is what I mean by reality."

His friend stood before him in the uncertain light. Michael?
Yes.
They embraced. How did you—
You forgot and left the back door open again. Just as you always did. I came in, helped myself to a piece of cheese, and waited.
Bastard! Scaring the shit out of me like that. He patted his shoulder. Michael looked thin, thin. You know, you could stand sideways and no one would know you were there. You ought to have had more of that cheese, you rat!
I guess you could get me for breaking and entering.
It's funny your appearing like this. I had a dream last night of an old friend but I couldn't decide who it was. Might have been you. Anyway, I had been estranged from the friend for some reason—some petty thing, I don't know what. I said to him, We're both getting old. But he didn't answer.
Maybe he had nothing to say.
I wanted to know what it meant.
The dream?
No, getting old.
It means nothing, you know. Just nothing. You get old. You die. Nothing.
I wish I could be certain even of that.
Pray for me.
I doubt that I'd know how. What an odd thing to ask.
Yes, I suppose it is. *O-r-a p-r-o n-o-b-i-s.* I'm afraid I can't stay long.
Where are you off to this time?
I don't know. Let's call it Argentina.
Argentina?
Yes. I have a situation there.
Teaching?
Yes, maybe. Learning is the real point, though. I'm tired of all this CRAP.
I thought you had tenure at L.A.
Time off for bad behavior. No one can live in L.A.
You have something permanent?
I don't know. We'll see. Anyway, I had this time in between.
Will you need a lift to the airport?
No, I have a car. A bit dented but mine. I thought I'd drop by and see you before—
Argentina's a long way off.
A lot of red meat there. Blood.
Will you try to look up Borges?
Hah—another dead man. I told you, I'm after blood.
Will a ham sandwich do?

I guess it'll have to. Whatever happened to your gourmet cooking?
Andrea got custody of the cooking. And of the politics. I lead a quiet life.
No hungry divorcees hoping for a real meal?
They'd need a real man for that. I'm tired.
You're real enough.
Maybe. You'd be surprised how much time the store takes up.
A man's work is his mistress.
I'm an old man. Anyway, where's *your* mistress?
Waiting for me in Argentina. I hope.
With dark and flashing eyes. Dances beautifully.
Probably blond and Jewish. I have a taste for contradictions. Speaking of which, my Jewish friend, where is that ham sandwich?...MMMMM, delicious. I don't know when I'll have such a sandwich again!

His friend had gone. They had embraced, exchanged good-byes. Michael had said, You know, the trouble with me is that I can only be certain I'm alive when I'm in the midst of a crisis. I manufacture them, I suppose. The words stayed in Abraham's mind: certain I'm alive. It was then that he remembered. Michael was not alive. He had been dead for several weeks. He remembered the letter, Dear Abraham, it is with great pain that we tell you...Michael had been buried in six feet of ground, he had been at the funeral himself. How could he have forgotten that? He felt a sudden tension, as if his friend's spirit had leapt into his body. It was not a sensation of invasion or violation but a sudden perception of new strength, as if he had somehow merged with another and yet had remained himself. Something had happened to his mind, to his understanding over the past few hours. It had been only a few hours ago (but *had* it been a few hours?) when he had KNOWN—known with great certainty—that his friend Michael was dead, that he had been killed in an automobile accident in New York City. *He had been visited by the spirit of his dead friend.* His mind felt suddenly stretched tight, then emptied of all the constructs he had placed there with such care. His friend's spirit "walking to and fro upon the earth." What could he possibly do to relieve him of such loneliness? Dar looked out over the endless sand. I can see her now endlessly watching. Night voices whispered to her. What good is that story she asked. It belongs to another time, to another person. What good can it be for Raguk and me.

No. The 4 people
we do have to have.
Last though.
I don't object to.
Reviewing at budget time.

But we do need to hire them
as perm.
employees
now. Turn-
over will
handle the problem

Various adjustments to be made between the obsessive quality of the beloved—the beloved in the head—and the actual person who can be touched, kissed.

Raguk opened his eyes. A horrible grayness was all around. He could not see properly. It was morning. Gray light flooded the room when he turned on the lamp. Where was Dar? Not here. He walked to the window and looked out. Nothing.

"Raguk..."

It was Dar's voice. Where was she? Outside?

He put on his coat.

"Dar...? Dar, where are you?"

Silence. Raguk could hear his own breathing.

"Dar..."

Lighting his lamp he stepped outside.

"Dar, where are you?"

"Raguk..."

Dreamlight. Nothing more. Nothing more than a dream... In the midst of the dream,   the tiger   *sprang!*

VILLANELLE

a poem of rage
—for Ivan Argüelles—

Villanelle, French, from the Italian *villanella,* an Italian rustic part song without accompaniment. Rustic dim. of *villano,* peasant, der. *villa.*

it is the word as power
                    as Dichtung
heir of Dante—living—
                              tongue leaps to rhythm
                                  to SPEECH—
empowered flowers flung against voidness
"where the small deer (for which read any small animal)
come to graze where her shadow has caused lush grass to grow"
in towers
song builds
in air
song
  living
            live words
                      flame
                          flare
                              leap into—
listen: "she was in deshabille confused looking around"
listen: "her page burning even as she breast-feeds the god"—
As we burn, burn—

Hour: sunset; fire retreating. Hour
Of thoughtfulness, sweet reverie.
Let us talk about the stupidity of publishers.

Let us talk about their vast and intricate MISUSE of powers
And of their equally vast and intricate, subtle and all-consuming STUPIDITY
At this hour: sunset; fire retreating; hour

When thought leaps to flower
When it is possible, possible, and sweet, to escape "the eye's tyranny"
Let us talk *now* about the stupidity of publishers!

Let us talk of the darkening of thought's tower
Or of the endless reverence for money
At *this* hour: sunset; fire retreating; hour

To remember the "pleasantries" of literary whores
Who stink up the mind's memories
Let us talk talk now about the stupidity of publishers

Let us take the rotting floor!
Let us remember the reviews and their duplicity!
At this hour: sunset; fire-retreating-hour—
Let us talk talk talk about the STUPIDITIES of PUBLISHERS!

He published her poem, and it was a good poem. But he published it on a page which contained much better poems, and so it looked *bad*

it is the word it is the word as power

listen: in the middle of the night the phone
RINGS

You wanna be God? Fail to show up at crucial points in people's lives!

—Dr. Ellen Kirschman, a psychologist who works with several police departments, said there is a "certain stress in working in a violent atmosphere" but the *most* stressful situation for an officer is after a shooting occurs. *(you believe in jesus? you believe in nothing. jesus is nothing)* "It is difficult to injure someone or to take another's life even when it is a righteous shoot," she said. "The public view that an officer takes it in stride is not the case." Kirschman said she believes "society at large is in a rage, especially in urban areas." *(there's something stinky in the base-ment)* She added that police in particular are "walking targets" for that rage because of the uniforms they wear and because people consider them symbols of the "powerful government" they perhaps blame for any problems they are having. "(Police) *(and poets)* have to pay attention to the officer safety issue. That's not being trigger happy," she said. "You can't get lulled into a sense of complacency."

I think it's about dichotomy, which is asserted at almost every line, every perception, and about the attempt to transcend dichotomy.

These pieces are a unit of sorts—with cross references—and they at once reveal & conceal a "savage scrutiny" centering on memory—

The Cape of Noah, she said, punning: *No escape!*

[to wait for someone, a loved one, to emerge
from a public place
the exact feeling of anxiety—anticipation—love—recognition—

the "war"
brings tears to the eyes—
how nice to see you,
                    alive

                              THIS IS GRACE, THE OPPOSITE OF DISGRACE

heir of Dante—living—
                              tongue leaps to rhythm
                                        TO SPEECH

                    (this is grace!)]

Grrr my name it is John Polkinghorne (and it is)
Grrr my name it is John Polkinghorne (AND IT IS)

Yes yes yes yes! But do get on with it! Delaying us, Cassie said indignantly, with all this talk about leaf-beet. —Yes, and I followed. But I had to wait for a porter to shift bags in the vestibule, and then I stepped aside and I got into the next car and I decided you'd gone ahead and I kept going and I thought I'd lost you and I hadn't caught a glimpse of you and I was going back to hover in your corridor some more and there wasn't any trace of anyone in there and you saw that for yourself and then I went away for a while and I got fed up and when they hunted for the pencil you know I never guessed it and the butt of a revolver cracked me over the head and I pitched forward and it wasn't much of a blow and the train lurched and my head lurched and my head

It was good to see you yesterday—& thanks again for the checks.

Hapax Legomenon
is a happy phenomenon

Hail to the (g)nomen on it
Pax to this *Hapax*
epic—an apex—
Praise to it—say: rex

—Folly the Feckless
to Argüelles the mixed Mex
whose verses are most max—
facts!

The rain poured down
A sudden shower
She's on the street—
wow! something to see!
She has forgotten
her umbrella
I've one I stole that day with me—
Mamselle, I say,
bowing politely, and—

There's only so much life, she says,
so much time,
What do you do with the rest of it?—

in the hidden
depths of you—

Someone's been reading me *The Education of Henry Miller.*
(pause, consideration of this possibility)
Adams. Someone's been reading you *The Education of Henry Adams.*
O yes, *Adams.*

His work is an attack on outworn esthetic fashions.
If they are outworn why should he bother to attack them?

The last few days have been difficult. They perhaps have the quality of "warnings."

she said no
meaning yes
(later) he said yes
meaning no

"Certainly there is a new vocabulary, and a new patterning possible to life." The Oedipal personality mounts an attack and asserts itself in terms of the "new." But all it really wishes to do is to *become the "old."* How does one arrive at the genuinely new? Somewhere in your mythic structures, I think, is the perception—and the conviction—that every genuine "dawn" involves a genuine "dark," and it is into this dark that your work has plunged—plunged with all your senses ("enlarged and numerous") ALERT

Fifty...a musical comedy of the mind!

Almost all the major poets of the West have been men who wrote about war What are the stylistic consequences of this—the consequences for poetic language? Even if the poem is not explicitly "about" war. There is an "explosive" quality to Hopkins' language. Does that have to do with the warrior tradition?

The measure of a life is not years lived but the impact that life has on others.

It's not young, she said, but it's young to *die.*

What was man? In what part of the conversation held amid shops & whistles
in which of those
metallic movements
dwelt the indestructible, the imperishable—life?

Que era el hombre?

The high rhetorical strategies of Neruda which I read in a Best Western Motel in Fort Bragg, California, because I am unable to sleep. Is it the heat? the wine we drank at dinner?

Take me—not because you want me but because I want it so much—

a multi-ethnic line—Asian, African, Euro Americans—

"Better Never Than Late" (a murder mystery) (This *life* as a murder mystery.)

The doctor said, "It's just cosmetic."
I said, "I know. But it's *my* cosmos."

What can be done to the phrases from Blake's "Holy Thursday"—altering them, punning upon them, changing everything—
    can be done (he said)

to the world—(oh yeah?)

Melt butter in a baking dish. Add sliced peaches. Mix pudding, milk, egg, peach juice, flour and 1/2 cup sugar. Pour over peaches. Bake at 350° for 35 minutes.

Lorene Hudgins, mother-in-law of Sandy Hudgins
Calling All Cooks
Telephone Pioneers of America
Alabama Chapter No. 34

OH DEATH OLD CAPTAIN IT IS TIME WEIGH ANCHOR *(raise ink!)*
THIS COUNTRY BORES US, DEATH—SPREAD SAIL

POUR OUT YOUR POISON SO IT COMFORTS US
THIS FIRE BURNS OUR BRAINS ANEW—WE WANT
WE WANT
TO PLUNGE INTO THE DEPTHS OF THE WATERS—HEAVEN OR HELL
WHO CARES
IN THE DEPTHS OF THE UNKNOWN TO FIND SOMETHING *NEW!*

Say, are they pigs? They just stuff like pigs. I never washed so damn many dishes in my life. All they did was eat, and all I did was eat, and I figured if she wanted these pigs to go to a lawyer, maybe they might help her. Got everything but running water.

Chard hoped that "Spaghetti" would leave everything to her, but when she discovered—

Does her death have to benefit anyone? Couldn't she have been killed simply because someone wanted to kill her? But that comes under the heading of homicidal mania, and the average maniac bent on homicide does not usually *lure his victim into the garage of a strange house, there to commit murder with a purloined pickax belonging to the local Chief of Police!*

there was a
barricade, a
barricade
on the horizon of
my Folie,
folly, Folie d'amour
dear—
and she had to

leave me,
after having said:
Thank you very much
and I watched her
                watched her
tiny as she was
go happily
TO THE COMPLETE OBLITERATION OF ANY THOUGHT OF ME!

how does one   raise it   he said
how does one   [click]   get it up

these are spaces
for thought,   she said
spaces—

for thought

Can you go on god damn it can you go on
in this error this
ever
underestimated
life

Yow! he said, I thought I had that baby—whew!—
under
            control
Baby replies: Fuck you, Mac.
Just keep
that Gerber's
coming

O, and the world, she said
O, and the world

"A man I shall call Joe has a family."
Someone I shall call a *man,* Joe, has a family.
A man I shall call "I" has a family.
A man I shall call "I" has a Joe.
A man has a family called "Chou."
A man called, "Joe, I have a family."
I shall call, "Man, Joe has a family."

A man I, shall Joe call a family?
A family shall I? Call Joe Sam?
A man I shall call Sam has a homily.
A man I shall call Sam writes a homily.
This family's homily. This family's a family.
O where is Joe? I shall call him, "Joe!"
"Hey, man," I shall call, "Sam's Ham had a family."
Man is a family. This critic's a man.
"Hey, man," I shall call, "Joe (Chou) has a family."
The Family of Man. A regular Chou.

The puzzle deepens when one considers that sediment on oceanic crust older than 20 million years stops increasing in thickness after it sinks to the depth where the calcareous ooze dissolves. Indeed, in many places the age of the oldest sediment is about the same as the volcanic layer on which it lies. It would therefore seem that almost all the deep-ocean sediment accumulates in narrow zones on the flanks of the mid-ocean ridges. If this is correct, it has yet to be explained.

Opposites throw light upon each other, and therefore it may be in place here to say that the proper opposite of the sublime is something which would not at first glance be recognized as such: *the charming* or *attractive.* We saw that the feeling of the sublime arises from the fact that something entirely unfavourable to the will becomes the object of pure contemplation so that such contemplation can be maintained only by persistently *turning away* from the will and transcending its interests. The charming or attractive draws the beholder away from the pure contemplation which is demanded by all apprehension of the beautiful because it necessarily excites this will by objects which directly appeal to it, and thus *he no longer remains pure subject of knowing, but becomes the needy and dependent subject of will.*

Every beautiful thing

Aw, Min—

–Therefore it seems to me that their malady specially concerns the MEMORY. It is not, indeed, a case of memory failing them entirely, for many of them know a great deal by heart, and sometimes recognize persons whom they have not seen for a long time. Rather is it a case of the thread of memory being broken, its continuous connexion being abolished, and of the impossibility of a uniformly coherent recollection of the past. Individual scenes of the past stand out correctly, just like the individual present; but there are gaps in their recollection that they fill up with fictions. These are either always the same, and so become fixed ideas; it is then a fixed mania or melancholy; or they are different each

time, momentary fancies; it is then called folly, *fatuitas*. This is the reason why it is so difficult to question a mad person about his previous life-history when he enters an asylum. In his memory the true is for ever mixed up with the false. Although the immediate present is correctly known, it is falsified through a fictitious connexion with an imaginary past. Mad people therefore consider themselves and others as identical with persons who live merely in their fictitious past. Many acquaintances they do not recognize at all, and, in spite of a correct representation or mental picture of the individual actually present, they have only false relations of this to what is absent. If the madness reaches a high degree, the result is a complete absence of memory; the mad person is then wholly incapable of any reference to what is absent or past, but is determined solely by the whim of the moment in combination with fictions that in his head fill up the past. In such a case, we are then not safe for one moment from ill-treatment or murder, unless we constantly and visibly remind the insane person of superior force.

why didn't the fish die? (gate)
why did he die? (pelvis)
why didn't the fish die?
why did he die?

"there are plenty of things   of interest here
if only one could take the time
to see them"

there are plenty of things
                    of interest here if only
one could take the time
                              to see them

SUPPLIANT   GULLS!

Hitherto, in all his journeys, he had never let himself go out of sight of home, for the dreary building, after all, was home—he remembered no other; but now he felt sick of the very look of his tower, with its round smooth walls and level battlements—

Dear J—

It was nice to talk with you on the phone. (Harvard)

I hope that your rather precipitous exposure to "What Jack Actually Thinks" wasn't too depressing! (Yale) I often find myself at odds with what "everyone"—or at least a sizeable number of people!—seems to think.

(Princeton) At first this was a problem, a difficulty. (Brown) Later, I think, it became a source of strength. (Cornell)

only a few
days, a week
perhaps, to
live, at this
extremity—
a life begun,
over, as
at the turn
of
a line—"She is terrified, terrified"—
projects, futurity, *the shapes of living*—
gone...

The chair is thinking to itself:.....

WHERE? *In one of its parts? Or outside its body; in the air around it? Or* *not* anywhere *at all? But then what is the difference between this chair's saying something to itself and another one's doing so, next to it?—But then how is it with man: where does* he *say things to himself? How does it come about that this question seems senseless...whereas the question* where *the chair talks to itself seems to demand an answer.—The reason is: we want to know* how *the chair is supposed to be like a human being; whether, for instance, the head is at the top of the back and so on.*

What is it like to say something to oneself; what happens here?—How am I to explain it? Well, only as you might teach someone the meaning of the expression *"to say something to oneself." And certainly we learn the meaning of* that *as children.—Only no one is going to say that the person who teaches it to us tells us 'what takes place.'*

this pain is partly the pain *of* uncertainty, I sd—& at the same time, an extremely strong intellectual *response* to that condition. These are all—or for the most part—"rush" poems, poems which seek to involve us in their own quick motion as the mind casts around from one thing to another, seeking—in its drive towards revelation, towards self-awareness—analogues for its own whirling condition.

—Self-consciousness

is committed he sd to an endlessly problematical *knowing*, a state which has, finally, no firm ground other than its own procedures, a condition which remains enormously active (& indeed, assertive) but at the same time enormously

"uncertain"

THE DESCENT INTO HELL & DARKNESS & THE NEED FOR "MEHR LICHT" are primal images, gestures. Song allows us to contemplate horrors & yet remain sane. It places the horrific thing directly in front of us, we see it all, & clearly, yet, because of the song, it *cannot* harm us. Song empties the terrible of its terror, annihilates *content*, yet leaves us with a "sweetness" that is certainly close to if it is not precisely a state of grace, a Buddhistic emptiness. Song seems to distance us from the world at the same time that it brings the world to us, with all its "news." Song's "sweetness" allows us a certain innocence in the midst of the inferno. Shhhhh, it says to the horrors, there's nothing going on here, only someone humming a tune.

"Off we go!" cried he. "Anywhere, so that I am away from here, and out into the world." "Gee-up! gee-up!" cried Prince Dolor in great excitement. "This is as good as riding a horse."

And he patted his cloak and tossed his head back and forth to meet the fresh breeze and pulled his coat collar up tight and his hat down as he felt the wind grow keener and colder—colder than anything he had ever known. *What did it matter.* As he spoke, the cloak, as if seized suddenly with a new idea, bounded forward and went skimming through the air, faster than the very fastest railway train. *N'importe où, hors du monde*, wrote Baudelaire. Anywhere, anywhere, out of this world!

—What does it mean therefore to "SEND IMAGINATION FORTH
UNDER THE DAY'S DECLINING LIGHT?"

There are a number of ways to describe the art it presented, but in much of that art one senses, as one senses in a considerable amount of Beat Generation art, *the perception of the infinite capacities of the mind*, and, beyond that, the perception of the joy of exercising those capacities.

In April, 1962, Paul Reps, author of *Zen Flesh, Zen Bones*, appeared at the Batman Gallery in San Francisco. Reps was announced with considerable fanfare—"Mr. Reps is well known in the Orient as the wandering bird, poet, and sumi artist...His works have been reproduced in such magazines as *Horizon* and *Between Worlds*, and have been exhibited at Pomona College. The present show is the first time these calligrams have been made available for sale through a gallery. Mr. Reps has been an authority on zen [*sic*] since the 1930s," etc.—and the show received a favorable review from Alfred Frankenstein. Here is a passage from Reps' transcription of "10 Bulls" as published in *Zen Flesh, Zen Bones*:

an article

Whip, rope, person, and bull—all merge in No-Thing.
This heaven is so vast no message can stain it.

How many a snowflake exist in a raging fire?
Here are the footprints of the patriarchs.

Comment: Mediocrity is gone. Mind is clear of limitation. I seek no state of enlightenment. Neither do I remain where no enlightenment exists. Since I linger in neither condition, eyes cannot see me. If hundreds of birds strew my path with flowers, such praise would be meaningless.

In the West, such a conception of the mind can be found in the Romantic understanding of the Imagination. (One thinks of the bohemian Shelley's of the early 1800's as not so far removed from the bohemians of San Francisco.) It is a naming of mind as, essentially, infinite. In one of the climactic passages of *The Renaissance*, Walter Pater wrote that "The base of all artistic genius is the power of conceiving humanity in a new, striking way, of putting a happy world of its own creation in place of the meaner world of common days, of generating around itself an atmosphere with a novel power of refraction, selecting, transforming, recombining the images it transmits, according to the choice of the imaginative intellect. In exercising this power, painting and poetry have a choice of subject almost unlimited." Such "power" was clearly evidenced by the artists who functioned in and around the Batman Gallery in the fifties and early sixties in San Francisco—particularly the artists associated with "assemblage." "When I looked at those early pieces [of Jay DeFeo's]," Michael McClure writes, "I was happy to be in San Francisco and not Paris. That was 1954." And again from Pater: *The demand of the intellect is to feel itself alive.* ("The Mind, that Ocean where each kind / Does streight its own resemblance find; / Yet it creates, transcending these, / Far other Worlds, and other Seas")

"I think my body has lasted this long because I've taken years off in the past," she said, "but my body isn't going to put up with this much longer. When I was in Cuba, I realized the pain is worthwhile. Meeting Fidel Castro was great and so is winning. When I won, I saw in blazing capital letters 'I DID IT' with the emphasis on the 'I.' It was a great feeling."

John Marshall quickened his pace yesterday when he saw two reporters trying to intercept him between the practice field and the locker room. "I've really got no time. I'm late for a meeting now," the San Francisco 49ers' defensive line coach said.

Actually, Marshall is always willing to talk—

Dear S—:

I am getting the feeling that you don't want to do this.

You were supposed to be at my house at 11 a.m. this morning to do a radio show. I'm here with your books, poems, statement on the nature of poetry, and my Spanish dictionary, but, for the second time, no S—.

On the oldtime radio show, *The Lone Ranger*, the actor playing Tonto (an Irishman, a Shakespearian actor) would get so bored at times he would fall asleep. The actor playing The Lone Ranger would then have to do *both* parts: "What do you think of *that*, Tonto?" "Hmmmm, hmmmm, kemo sabe." I haven't quite reached that point with you yet, but soon, soon... "Why did you write that poem, S—?" "Well, Jack—"

(IN THE CONSUBSTANTIAL NATURE OF THIS DARK!)
this, he sd, is the nature of LANGUAGE—

(angrily) *Aren't "most" men not in touch with their feelings?*

I'm not one of them & I know plenty of men who weren't.
You tell me I'm an exception, but I don't think so. I was
aware of the Men Shouldn't Show Their Feelings, They Should
Be Tough, Men Should Do This, Men Should Do That kind of
thing as I grew up. I thought it was silly because it didn't
seem to apply. No thoughtful person—and there were & are
plenty of thoughtful persons—needed to take it seriously.

To put it another way: The myth of the "rough tough"
male was over & it was perfectly clear that it was over.
Even John Wayne was always "feeling things"—compassion for
buddies in war films, love, etc. It perhaps had been *one*
(not the only) way of being male in our culture but, really,
nobody seemed to believe in it anymore.

What seems to be happening *now* is that we are taking
this stick figure, knocking it over, & congratulating our-
selves at our bravery in doing so. Why should we do that?
Well, at one point the stick figure of the Tough Man might
have been taken (with qualifications) as the Norm, the image
of what a man should be. By my time it was no problem for me
to knock it over. *But if I knocked that over what else might
I knock over?* What other stick figures were there just
waiting for an inquiring mind to knock them over—in the
realm of religion, for example, or in social relations?
That, I think, was the real question. How could the Status
Quo deal with that?

Well, says the Status Quo, let's make a *big deal* about

getting beyond the myth of the Tough Man. Nobody believes in it anyway so we aren't losing anything. Let's congratulate men on *not becoming the stick figure* (which they weren't in much danger of doing anyway). We'll make such a nice fuss about that that they won't ask other, more difficult questions. Let's keep men asleep. Remember that the Tough Man not only didn't feel, he didn't *think.* He went along with the way things were. What we need is a *new* image of man which will do the same thing. We'll create the *aware* man, the man in touch with his feelings. Only we'll make certain that he isn't *too* aware...That way we can make a great pretense of change without having to change anything at all, without having to lose a thing.

(And what, she said, about Arnold Schwarzenegger??)

be editor of the dead!
tell the dead
which verses will be saved, which not
be editor of the dead
let the dead throng to tell you
how they worked this poem over & over again until they got it right
or how it came
so suddenly
they distrusted it
or how the words
flowed in an unusual & satisfying way
or how they are experiencing just now a temporary
BLOCKAGE
be their editor
who come breathless
to meet you & greet you & give you
their
poetry

-in the special light
the mind casts
the special light
of sweetness clarity and anger [charity!]
in this
light
this

sweetest
comprehension
you, or I
casting
looks, words
at nothing other than ourselves
at nothing other than
the world
emptied
of everything but   lightlightlightlightlightlightlight
how are we to speak?
song
   clarifies & empties
in   *this*   light   love
lingers, asking
everything
as a child asks
everything
all-powerful
enunciation
sweetness

. *sweeter than the honey*
   gathered by the bee .

(gesture, towards him) "you know what I mean fellow traveler in music"

WORDS & BOOKS; POETRY & WRITING

speech delivered by my wife Adelle and me to
the San Francisco Bay Area Book Fair 11/4/90

At the conclusion of *Wen Fu*, his treatise on the art of writing, Lu Chi, born in the Yangtze delta in 261 A.D. and author of the first book of criticism in the Chinese language, writes about writing:

> Consider the use of letters, for all principles demand them.
> Though they travel a thousand miles & more, nothing in the world can stop them; they traverse ten thousand years.
> Look at them one way, and they clarify laws for the future; look at them another, and they provide models from old masters.
> The art of letters has saved governments from certain ruin and propagates proper morals.
> Through letters there is no road too distant to travel, no idea too confusing to be ordered.
> It comes like rain from clouds; it renews the vital spirit.

(I quote from Sam Hamill's translation, which makes no attempt to reproduce the rhyme of the original.)

Is this true? Has the art of letters "saved governments from certain ruin" and propagated "proper morals"? (One might ask Jesse Helms about that one.) Does literature—letters—come "like rain from clouds"? Does it renew "the vital spirit"? What does all this propaganda mean?

In the section called "Beginning," Lu Chi writes of the poet,

> Eyes closed, he hears an inner music; he is lost in thoughts and questions—
> His spirit rides to the eight corners of the universe, his mind a thousand miles away.
> And then the inner voice grows clearer as objects become defined.
> And he pours forth the essence of words, savouring their sweetness.

What does the "art of writing" have to do with having your eyes *closed?* What is an "*inner* music"? Lu Chi's poet, at least at his "beginning," is alienated from the world, distanced, "lost in thoughts and questions." He is not in any way a "performer." Words arise out of the intensity of his subjectivity—imaged here as the magical ability to travel enormous distances. We recognize him easily because we have so many examples from our own culture:

> His flashing eyes, his floating hair!
> Weave a circle round him thrice,
> And close your eyes with holy dread,
> For he on honey-dew hath fed,
> And drunk the milk of Paradise.
>
> *Kubla Khan*

Coleridge too speaks of closed eyes. Why should writing, which depends upon vision, be associated with such a state? The Homeric singer, on the other hand, has not closed his eyes. He has been blinded by the very Muse whose bidding he does. In the eighth Book of *The Odyssey*, Alcinous says, "Let some one bid to the gathering our divine minstrel Demodocus, to whom the God has given such gift of music that he charms his hearers with every song to which his heart is moved":

> The herald came to hand leading the beloved minstrel, whom the Muse did especially love: yet had her gifts to him been mixed, both good and evil. She had taken from him the sight of his eyes, and given him a power of harmony. Pontonous backed a silver-studded throne against a tall pillar in the midst of the feasters and set it for the musician and put him on it; then hung the resonant lyre on a peg above him and guided his hand to the place, so that later he might know to reach it down. Beside him he set a food basket and a goodly table and a wine-cup ready, that he might drink as his spirit prompted. The company plunged hands into the bounty provided, until they had satisfied their lust for drink and meat. Then the Muse pricked the musician on to sing of the great deeds of heroes, as they were recounted in verses whose fame had already filled the skies...
>
> Of this was the song of the very famous minstrel: but Odysseus with two strong hands drew the broad purple cloak over his head to hide his goodly face. He was ashamed to let the tears well from his deep-set eyes publickly before the Phaeacians. Each time the divine singer broke off his song Odysseus dashed away the tears, freed his head from the cloak, and poured from his loving cup a libation to the God.
>
> (trans. Col. T.E. Lawrence)

The contrast could not be greater. Homer's "beloved minstrel," like the poet of Lu Chi's *Art of Writing*, bursts into song, but he is not listening to "an inner music"; he is not "lost in thoughts and questions"; despite his blindness, he is directed outward, towards his audience; he is, precisely, performing. Indeed, he is not even necessarily the author of the poem he is performing, a poem which Homer describes as dealing with "the great deeds of heroes, as they were recounted *in verses whose fame had already filled the skies.*" The author of the poem is not specifically mentioned, but that doesn't seem to matter very much. If anything, the Muse is the author of the poem—as the Muse is certainly the inspiration of the poet. Odysseus doesn't drink to the wonderful poet who composed the poem which the "divine singer" is reciting but pours "from his loving cup a libation to the God." Song, it seems, originates in mystery, but it is not the mystery of selfhood, as it is in Lu Chi. Lu Chi (born 261 A.D.) and Homer (born, perhaps, 850 B.C.) both present us with an image of the poet—and they are in a way rather similar images. The poet in the act of speaking his poetry is definitely something to see. But Lu Chi's image represents precisely the *transformation* of the image Homer gives us. The divinely inspired poet for Lu Chi is suddenly thrust inwards and away from his external circumstances:

> Eyes closed, he hears an inner music; he is lost in thoughts and questions—
> His spirit rides to the eight corners of the universe, his mind a thousand miles away.

His eyes are closed because the external world is no longer present to him. The Muse, on the other hand, thrusts the Homeric singer outward towards his audience as his "power of harmony" (which is no "inner music" but dependent in part upon the very real "resonant lyre" that hangs "on a peg above him") moves Odysseus to tears. He does not transport his auditors "to the eight corners of the universe" but reminds them of their life; tells them what it means to be human as he sings "the great deeds of heroes." He does not pour forth "the essence of words" but stirs specific memories in his audience. As the text makes clear, Odysseus is listening to events in which he has participated; he is listening to his own life.

Is the poet public or is he private? Do his words move outward to the world or inward towards a pure subjectivity, an "essence of words"? Are both these stances myths—and, if they are, what are they expressing? What do they have to do with *Wen Fu,* "the art of writing"?

Writing about writing in his great book, *Interfaces of the Word,* Father Walter J. Ong refers to "the indissoluble alliance which writing and print have with death, the great separator." Writing turns performer and listener, who are necessarily physically, immediately present to one another, into author and reader, who are necessarily not—who are, as if by death, separated:

> Even by Jane Austen's time...the problem of the reader's role in prose narrative was by no means entirely solved. Nervousness regarding the role of the reader registers everywhere in the "dear reader" regularly invoked in fiction well through the nineteenth century. The reader had to be reminded (and the narrator, too) that the recipient of the story was indeed a reader—not a listener, not one of the crowd, but an individual isolated with a text.

"Not a listener, not one of the crowd, but an individual isolated with a text." The isolation of Lu Chi's poet is indeed linked to "the art of writing." Writing for both writer and reader tends towards isolation—towards separateness, towards "privacy." I need to be alone so I can write. I need to get away in order to finish my novel. The image of Lu Chi's poet is the image, by now enormously hackneyed, of the sensitive, isolated, perhaps even "misunderstood" individual—a figure whose isolation mirrors the isolation of the reader alone with his book. The reader's eyes are not in fact closed, as the poet's are, but they are nevertheless turned away from the world: they are focused on a *book*, not on the world around him. In the mirror of his text, Lu Chi's words apply as much to the reader as they do to the poet:

> Eyes closed, he hears an inner music; he is
> lost in thoughts and questions—
> His spirit rides to the eight corners of the
> universe, his mind a thousand miles away.*

The figure of the heroic poet listening to "an inner music" is a mythologizing of the act of reading. What has reading to do with poetry? What happens when, as Eric A. Havelock puts it, "the muse learns to write"? The Homeric poet's blindness is an indication that he has nothing at all to do with writing. There was no Braille in Homer's day. At its beginnings, poetry is rooted in physical presence and in sounds, and, whatever the labyrinthine complexities of its history—and they are many—it always maintains some sort of connection to its purely oral past. "In a shell of murmurings," wrote Robert Duncan in the 1960s,

> rimed round,
> sound-chamberd child
> *Bending the Bow*

"Well then," said Socrates to Phaedrus,

> are we able to imagine another sort of discourse, a legitimate brother of our bastard [writing]? How does it originate? How far is it better and more powerful in nature?

---

* Writing is of special importance to the Chinese. Father Ong: "Classical Chinese is a very special case because of its non-alphabetic character system of writing. Chinese is conventionally spoken of as a language of various 'dialects' but is in fact a group of mutually unintelligible languages, each with its own subset of dialects, all of which languages and dialects use a system of writing consisting of tens of thousands of the same highly stylized pictures or 'characters,' allusively nuanced with an exquisite sophistication developed over the centuries. The K'anghsi dictionary of A.D. 1716 lists 40,545 characters. If two persons speaking 'dialects' of 'Chinese' so different that they cannot understand one another at all when they talk (thus really speaking different languages), will only write in Chinese characters what they are saying, each will be able to understand what the writer means, although when the reader reads it off in his own Chinese, the writer will not be able to understand what is being said" (*Interfaces of the Word*).

Phaedrus. What sort of discourse? What do you mean about its origin?
Socrates. A discourse which is inscribed with genuine knowledge in the soul of the learner; a discourse that can defend itself and knows to whom it should speak and before whom to remain silent.
Phaedrus. Do you mean the living, animate discourse of a man who really knows? Would it be fair to call the written discourse only a kind of ghost of it?
Socrates. Precisely.
(Plato, *The Phaedrus*)

Written discourse, writes Plato, is "only a kind of ghost" of "the living, animate discourse of a man who really knows." The shift from Socrates, who never wrote anything, to Plato, who was a writer, is the shift from an oral culture to a culture in which writing is of enormous importance. It is the beginning of the myth of subjectivity, of inwardness, a myth which finds its apotheosis in the conception of the "unconscious," a conception of an area of the mind so "subjective" that it is for the most part inaccessible. The history of this myth of subjectivity is bound up with the history of writing. Do we speak our words aloud as we write or read them or are we silent before the page? Just as there are areas of the mind which must be "read," "interpreted," "decoded" before they can be understood, so words—the products of our breaths and bodies—are hidden in the tangles of "letters."

The following poem, published by E.E. Cummings in 1935, is, literally, unspeakable:

```
                r-p-o-p-h-e-s-s-a-g-r
           who
a)s w(e loo)k
upnowgath
               PPEGORHRASS
                                    eringint(o-
aThe):l
        eA
           !p:
S                                a
               (r
                 .gRrEaPsPhOs)
                                     to
  rea(be)rran(com)gi(e)ngly
  ,grasshopper;
```

No Thanks

[Speakers are silent
while audience examines poem]

Cummings' poem brilliantly places us at the exact point at which letters turn into words. The struggle to see the grasshopper as it moves and leaps in the grass is mirrored by the struggle of our eyes to make sense —and words—

out of Cummings' disarranged letters. But it is an entirely visual struggle. r-p-o-p-h-e-s-s-a-g-r cannot be pronounced except as individual letters until one turns the letters around and perceives them to be "grasshopper." It is as far from the oral as a poem can be. *At a certain point in its history Western poetry takes the page, and "letters," as its primary mode of dissemination.* The ancestor of Cummings' poem is Stéphane Mallarmé's *Un Coup de Dès, A Throw of the Dice Will Never Abolish Chance*, a poem published in 1897. Mallarmé's poem marks the very first moment in which a modern poet *admits* that he is working with a page and that the page, even the entire book, can be used for expressive purposes. Beginning with that poem (which, as Mallarmé says, "has no precedent") modern poetry embarks upon an enormously important experiment, an experiment which continues into the present day, with *specifically visual experience.* Mallarmé not only accepts the silence and whiteness of the page as the primary means for the dissemination of his poetry, he makes active use of it. I cannot possibly enter into the historical ramifications of *Un Coup de Dès* but suffice it to say that that poem gives birth to an extraordinary series of experiments with typefaces, with white space, with patterns, with letters (as in Apollinaire as well as E.E. Cummings), with "field" techniques, with all sorts of *essentially visual phenomena.* In addition, poets begin to claim that their work is *grounded* in the visual, in "images," and for the first time it is possible to argue, as C. Day Lewis does in *The Poetic Image* (1947), that "imagery," not the "power of harmony," is the very basis of poetry. The intense visual focus on the book, which is necessary if reading is to occur at all, becomes the very theme and condition of poetry. The poem exists, as Cummings puts it very well, only "a)s w(e loo)k."

Yet this is by no means the end of the story. Writing is itself at this moment in a state of crisis. For the first time in its history, it finds itself *in competition* with other modes of expression. Our children, we complain, don't read enough. Literacy is declining. *For many years writing was the only way of preserving human speech*, but this is no longer the case. The tape or the phonograph record or the radio or the television can give you the exact sound of the person who is speaking. In his book, *The Muse Learns to Write*, Eric A. Havelock reflects upon the new interest in orality which has characterized much scholarship in the past 25 to 30 years. Why, he asks, "should...works produced simultaneously in three different countries have all involved themselves in the role of human language in human culture? Why, in particular, this focus on the spoken language in contrast to the written?" His answer is: "We had all been listening to the radio...." The electronic media have already changed the conditions of writing, though the exact nature of that change is not yet clear. We live, as Father Ong put it in 1977, in an "opening state of consciousness," a state in which even the nature of biography—the nature of what we believe it means to be human—may have to be reconsidered. Lu Chi's inward-looking poet, the type of the subjective man, may strike us as oddly old-fashioned. The figure of the Homeric singer, with its very different sense of personality structure, has been a haunting presence in modern literature, whether one speaks of James Joyce or W.B. Yeats or H.D. or Ezra Pound or Jack Kerouac or Judy Grahn. What are we likely to experience next? We don't know, but we have an intense sense that it is likely to be *different.*

SOURCES

The poems in *Adrift* are collage poems and quote from (and at times distort) a great many sources. Collage is, as Jerome Rothenberg has pointed out, "the great structuring device (& more) of early twentieth-century (= *modernist*) art, appearing there under a multiplicity of names: simultanism, vortex, montage, surreal or double or deep image, assemblage, perspective by incongruity, or plain 'collage'" (*Sulfur* 14, 1985). It is also a natural form for a multicultural sensibility—in my own case, Irish, Italian, American. For such a sensibility, identity itself is "collage."

A "chorus" in my work is a multivoiced piece. Many of these poems were written to be performed by my wife Adelle and me.
The sign } is an indication that passages are to be spoken simultaneously.

- "Sweeney Adrift"

This poem is a fantasia based on a medieval Irish poem called *Buile Suibhne. Buile Suibhne* was translated first by J.G. O'Keefe in 1913 as *Sweeney The Mad* and then by Seamus Heaney in 1984 as *Sweeney Astray.* My poem is not a translation, but I do use the Irish poem as the basis for themes and variations of my own. The opening quotation is from T.S. Eliot's "Sweeney Among the Nightingales." (Eliot's anti-Semitism has been noted, but he is equally prejudiced against the Irish.) Other sources: A. Irving Hallowell, *Bear Ceremonialism in the Northern Hemisphere;* Herbert Wendt, *Out of Noah's Ark;* Tony Moffeit's poem, "Those Who Speak Do Not Know Those Who Know Do Not Speak," *Oro Madre*, vol. 2, no. 3-4; Rhys Carpenter, *Folktale, Fiction and Saga in the Homeric Epics; Funk & Wagnalls Standard Dictionary of Folklore, Mythology, and Legend* (the article on the "Bear's Son"); Robert Lamberton's translation of Porphyry's essay, *On the Cave of the Nymphs;* Ivan Argüelles' poem, "Descending Paralysis"; Kathleen Hoagland, *1000 Years of Irish Poetry;* Ivan T. Sanderson, *The Continent We Live On*; Georges Norge, "Les Innocents" from *La Belle Saison* (I have translated only part of this poem); Jules Romains, *The Body's Rapture*, trans. by John Rodker; some of my own very early poetry; John Milton, *Paradise Lost*, Book VI; Alexis de Tocqueville, *Democracy in America*, the Henry Reeve text as revised by Francis Bower; Plato, *The Republic*, Books VI and VII (I used both the Jowett and the Rouse translations); Conrad Arensberg, *The Irish Countryman;* James Harkness' introduction to his translation of Michel Foucault's *This Is Not A Pipe;* Paul de Man's introduction to his *The Rhetoric of Romanticism.* The second passage in the epilogue was written while listening to Charlie Parker ("of birds / a harvest- / wealth-"). John Anson is a friend of mine who published a sequence of a hundred roundels, *Sessions and Surroundings: A Century of Roundels.* I responded to his sequence with my one. My proper name is "John" and my mother's name was a variant of "Ann," so I am in a sense "John, Ann's son."

- "Chorus: SON(G)"

Wordsworth's preface to the second edition of *Lyrical Ballads;* Paul de Man's last letter to Jacques Derrida, quoted in Derrida's *Mémoires;* Tákis Sinópoulos, "The Sea," *Landscape of Death;* John R. Pierce, *The Science of Musical Sound;* Georges Brassens' song, "Tempête Dans Un Bénitier" is from his Philips album, *Don Juan;* Craig Williamson, *A Feast of Creatures; English and Scottish Popular Ballads*, ed. Helen Child Sargent and George Lyman Kittredge; Jules Romains, *The Body's Rapture*, trans. by John Rodker; Roman Jakobson, *Six Lectures on Sound and Meaning; SF Chronicle* article about then President Reagan; A.J. Arberry, *Mystical Poems of Rumi.* The passage beginning "articulation of sound" is based on phrases from the beginning of Coleridge's essay, "On Poesy Or Art." The doggerel poem, "The Subject Was Rocks," has a story behind it: Many years ago, a Berkeley friend of mine was involved in a disastrous love affair. At its conclusion, in despair, he hurled a rock through a window of his girl friend's house, damaging the window but nothing else. Much later, in Cambridge, MA, he met a friend of this girl friend's and had a conversation with her. He wrote to tell me, "The subject was rocks." My friend would have heard—as I do—a reference to testicles in the word "rocks." (Cf. "the family jewels.")

• "Chorus: *Darkness. The light comes slowly.*"
Charles Darwin, *The Origin of Species;* Albert Einstein, *Relativity;* William H. Prescott, *History of the Conquest of Mexico;* Hans Christian Andersen, *The Fairy Tale Of My Life* (the person fearful of appearing "out of Sweden" is Jenny Lind).

• "Prose For Two Voices"
This was written after seeing *The Pumpkin Eater* in Ellen Drori's Berkeley film class.

• "Turning Forty"
The opening section of the poem is not included here. "Bus Ride" contains quotations from *The Autobiography of Giambattista Vico*, trans. by Max Harold Fisch and Thomas Goddard Bergin. A "word box" is a cigar box—in this case, Shakespeare Cigars—in which children place words in order to learn them. Sources of the concluding section are: Montague Summers, *The History of Witchcraft; SF Chronicle* (the now defunct comic strip, "Apt. 3G"); D.H. Lawrence, "The Ship Of Death;" Ralph Waldo Emerson, "Nature"; David H. Greene, *An Anthology of Irish Literature; The Golden Bough*; an encyclopedia article on exotic fish; H.T.F. Rhodes, *The Satanic Mass;* Vico's *Autobiography;* Alfred North Whitehead, *Process and Reality.* The typos in the passage from Whitehead—beginning, "There is nothing self-contradictory" – are not errors but intended. Stephen W. Hawking suggests that what we call "time" is the same as what we call "entropy."

• "Fifty"
"Fifty" has a number of popular song titles scattered throughout. There are also quotations from newspaper articles which appeared in the *Oakland Tribune* and the *SF Chronicle.* The "garden" passages, sometimes altered, are from various articles appearing in *The American Gardener, A Sampler*, ed. Allen Lacy. Other sources: The opening line of Antonin Artaud's radio play, *Pour En Finir Avec Le Jugement De Dieu*, and a comment about the play from the record jacket in which it came; a comment about Robert Benchley from Gerald Nachman of the *SF Chronicle*; a letter from New York sent me by someone for whom I had done a small favor; the comic strip, "Dr. Rex Morgan"; Ean Begg, *The Cult of the Black Virgin;* L. Adams Beck, *The Ninth Vibration and Other*

Stories; a statement of Heidegger's, which I altered slightly and which was quoted by Nicholas Rand in "The Political Truth of Heidegger's 'Logos': Hiding in Translation," *PMLA* (May, 1990); a letter from Robert Duncan to Mary Fabilli, quoted in Ekbert Faas, *Young Robert Duncan: Portrait of the Poet As Homosexual In Society* (Mary tells me she never received the letter); a letter I wrote to James Broughton in which I mention one of Larry Eigner's typos; my horoscope as it appeared in the *Oakland Tribune.* "The world is damned" is a sentiment I echo from Jake Berry's amazing poem, *Brambu Drezi.* The "highly sounded" piece referred to is "A-11" by Louis Zukofsky. I have also quoted a few words from a KPFA radio show—a special program about Clayton Eshleman which Benjamin Lindgren and I presented a few years ago.

- "Villanelle"

"Villanelle" contains a few quotations from Ivan Argüelles' long poem, *Pantograph*, one section of which is called "Hapax Legomenon." (The concluding line of "Villanelle" contains a quotation from Argüelles' poem.) "The eye's tyranny" is a version of a phrase used by Peter Redgrove in an interview appearing in the English magazine, *Poetry: Magazine of the Poetry Society* (June, 1987). "Certainly there is a new vocabulary..." is from a letter Redgrove sent me. "A man I shall call Joe..." is from the poet/translator Sam Hamill's book of essays, *A Poet's Work.* I have translated the concluding lines of Baudelaire's "Le Voyage"—though I have rather fancifully taken Baudelaire's phrase, "levons l'ancre," to be a pun on "levons l'encre," raise ink. (Baudelaire himself took the phrase, "anywhere out of this world," from Thomas Hood's poem, "The Bridge of Sighs." The phrase is sometimes wrongly attributed to E.A. Poe.) Other sources: *SF Chronicle* newspaper articles; parts of Georges Brassens' song, "La Parapluie," my translation; Alice Tilton, *Cold Steal* (often with considerable alteration); Pablo Neruda, "The Heights of Macchu Picchu" (I consulted translations by both Nathaniel Tarn and Kate Flores); H.W. Menard, "The Deep-Ocean Floor" in *Continents Adrift, Readings from* Scientific American, with introductions by J.Tuzo Wilson; a recollection of Wallace Beery in the film, *Min and Bill; The Little Lame Prince* by Miss Mulock; Ludwig Wittgenstein, *Philosophical Investigations,* trans. by G.E.M. Anscombe (I have altered the passage); W.B. Yeats' poem, "The Tower" (the line is slightly misquoted); Arthur Schopenhauer, *The World As Will and Representation,* translated by E. F. J. Payne (again a somewhat altered version); my introduction to Elizabeth Claman's book, *Peripheral Visions* (the phrase, "savage scrutiny" is hers); Andrew Marvell's "The Garden"; a paper I wrote on the Batman, a San Francisco art gallery which flourished from 1960-1965; a Josephine Baker song, "Pretty Little Baby," by "Silvers/Baker & Bernie." The suggestion about Hopkins seems a little more probable if one remembers his poem, "Yes. Why do we all, seeing of a soldier, bless him?"

§

Design and typography by Robert Frazier
Printed by BookMasters, Inc.
on acid-free paper

§

A companion tape to this book is available from Pantograph Press, containing performances by Jack and Adelle Foley as well as an hour-long poetry and jazz radio program with Jack Foley, saxophonist Glenn Spearman, and bassist Ben Lindgren.

OTHER TITLES FROM PANTOGRAPH

Ivan Argüelles, *Hapax Legomenon* (1-880766-04-3) $8.95.

Ivan Argüelles, *"That" Goddess* (1-880766-00-0) $8.95.

Denyse Du Roi, *Filmmaking* (1-880766-01-9) $8.95.

Andrew Joron, *Science Fiction* (1-880766-02-7) $8.95.

Andrew Joron, editor, *Terminal Velocities: An Anthology of Speculative Poetry* (1-880766-03-5) $11.95.

Laurie Price, *Except for Memory* (1-880766-06-X) $8.95.

Order from Small Press Distribution, 1814 San Pablo Avenue, Berkeley, California 94702.